BREAKING YOUR
COMFORT ZONES

Also by Joey O'Connor

Whadd'ya Gonna Do? 25 Secrets for Getting a Life
Where Is God When . . . 1001 Answers to Questions
  Students Are Asking
You're Grounded for Life! and 49 Other Crazy Things
  Parents Say

BREAKING YOUR COMFORT ZONES

*And 49 Other Extremely Radical Ways
to Live for God*

JOEY O'CONNOR

Fleming H. Revell
A Division of Baker Book House Co
Grand Rapids, Michigan 49516

©1996 by Joey O'Connor

Published by Fleming H. Revell
a division of Baker Book House Company
P.O. Box 6287, Grand Rapids, MI 49516-6287

Printed in the United States of America

Library of Congress Cataloging-in-Publication Data

O'Connor, Joey, 1964–
    Breaking your comfort zones : and 49 other extremely radical ways to live for God / Joey O'Connor.
    p. cm.
    ISBN 0-8007-5584-7 (pbk.)
    1. Teenagers—Conduct of life. 2. Teenagers—Religious life. I. Title.
BV4531.2.036 1996
248'.3—dc20   95-37517

To the three most beautiful, wild, wonderful women in my life . . . Krista, Janae, and Ellie. Your tender hearts, sparkling smiles, and spontaneous laughter are more valuable to me than anything else. I am the richest man alive.

CONTENTS

FOREWORD

Maybe you've seen the painting of Jesus that hangs in lots of Sunday school rooms—the one in which he's standing there holding a cuddly little lamb in his arms. The picture does a pretty good job of showing the tenderness of Jesus. The image is warm, safe, comfortable.

I like that picture. But it shows just *one* side of Jesus. I'd like to see more. Like a portrait of Jesus on the mountaintop, telling Satan (who's just offered him the world) to take a hike (Matt. 4:8–10). Or an action shot of Christ flipping over sales tables at the temple-turned-flea-market (Matt. 21:12–13). Or maybe this one (but I'm not sure I could stomach it): a picture of Jesus touching a person deformed and consumed by leprosy (Matt. 8:2–3).

These moments, and a hundred others, show Jesus stepping out of what was comfortable, pushing life and love and faith to the limit.

But I don't really need to see these moments captured on canvas. I see pictures like this all the time—in living color—in Joey O'Connor's life. Once my student and always my friend, Joey creates self-portraits with his faith that reveal the message in these Scripture passages. What's more, his students look at his life and do the same thing: They step out of their comfort zones to live the radical Christian life.

Now it's your turn. Take a look at these snapshots of Joey and his students stepping out of their comfort zones and into the radical faith Jesus showed us. Then take these steps in your own life. Someone you know is watching you, waiting for a picture that shows them how.

Todd Temple
Del Mar, California

INTRODUCTION

You and I have grown up being told not to break things. We've been warned, forewarned, prewarned, admonished, cautioned, yelled at, and threatened not to break: China dishes. Crystal vases. Dad's favorite golf club. Pearl necklaces. Beautiful, mostly useless things in expensive department stores. Orthodontic retainers. Windows. Antiques. Keys in locks. Eyeglasses. Anything in the house. Toys. Arms. Legs. Noses. And fish tanks.

As little, mischievous children, we have endured polite threats in nice stores with little, stupid signs, "Nice to touch, Nice to hold, If you break it, consider it sold." Though that's what the sign said, when that expensive, ugly glass sculpture mysteriously slid off the shelf and shattered into a zillion pieces, the store manager actually had something very different to say: "How many times have I had to tell you &#!# kids to keep your &#!#s hands off of my &#!#s merchandise? Who's going to pay for this?"

Not only have we been warned again and again not to break things like family heirlooms, hamster cages, and hula hoops (Okay, it's pretty tough to break a hula hoop, but have you ever tried to hula with a bent hoop?), we just so happen to live in a world where things constantly get broken. We're sternly told, "Don't touch or break anything!" But we know things always break. Try to fix that paradoxical contradiction! So, from the instant when the water breaks in our mother's womb, you and I head out to live in a world of impossible standards and expectations.

I have very vivid memories of things breaking during my childhood. There was the daughter of a family friend who broke the plate glass window in my bedroom by running right through it. There was the time when, in a fit of rage, I broke every single racing car model I ever made. (I had about twenty really cool models. I later regretted that stupid maneuver!) I remember watching adults break things I wasn't supposed to break and then, I also heard them say words I wasn't allowed to say.

The absolute worst thing I ever broke was the treasured, sacred war spear of my YMCA Indian Guide tribe. Every father-and-son duo was told to carve a certain section of our tribe's seven-foot-tall war spear. Each week, a different father and son got to take the spear home so they could carve their part of it. It was a sacred privilege for an eight-year-old. One not to be taken lightly.

While other dads and sons carved, chiseled, and painted elaborate patterns, eagles, bears, and other sacred Indian symbols, the only section I cared about was the tip. I wanted to carve a sharp tip on the spear because that was the part that really made the sucker fly. The sharp tip was the most important part for piercing prey and tribal enemies.

It was finally our turn to take home the sacred war spear. Since he knew how badly I wanted to carve the tip by myself, my dad left the whole task up to me. He gave me a sharp knife, and I began to whittle away at the tip every day after school. I finished my sacred war spear tip a few days later and now was ready to launch it into the great white clouds of L.A.

Tying a colored beach towel between two flexible juniper trees, I placed the sacred war spear in the middle of the beach towel catapult and pointed the sharp tip toward the sky. Pulling the spear back with all the Indian warrior strength I could muster, I released it at the catapult's maximum tension point. *CRAAACK!*

The spear flew approximately two feet forward, didn't even come close to clearing the clothesline, crashed onto the cement, and snapped into two large pieces. *Oh no!* I cried to myself. *I'm going to be banished from the tribe! I broke the sacred war spear!*

Todd Temple, my high school youth director and youth ministry mentor, always told me, "Things break, bodies bruise, and personalities clash. Remember this and you'll be able to handle just about anything." I've never forgotten those important words of wisdom. They have always been a reminder to me that I live in a broken world. A world where even sacred war spears shatter into pieces. A whole world separated from a loving God because of a broken command. A world where lives without God are broken because of the fall. A broken, fallen world.

Since you've always been told not to break things, yet you live in a broken world, the tragic result is that it's really hard to figure out what you can or can't break. Some things in life are meant to be broken, but nobody's really explained or shown you what to break or why. In fear of being reprimanded, you decide it's a whole lot safer to no longer take any risks. Apathy replaces a sense of adventure for life. A foreboding sense of danger shadows your every move. *I'd better not touch, try, or change anything . . . I might break it.* The result is the development of an invisible, malignant growth on your heart called a "comfort zone." It's a thick, fat layer of protective insulation that keeps you from trying, touching, or changing anything about your life. Like the things that really need changing: Bad habits. Negative thinking. Treating others like primordial goo. Abusing drugs and alcohol. The list goes on and on.

A comfort zone keeps you in control, safely away from others and free from making a positive difference in anyone's life. It appears to keep you from getting into trouble, but what a comfort zone really does is keep you from growing and enjoying life. A comfort zone keeps you from breaking the things in your life that really need to be broken and tossed away.

A spiritual comfort zone is that tough, isolated wall of a cocoon where you can't be bothered by anything or anyone. Even God. It's a selfish little space where you can zone out, veg out, space out, and turn into a spiritual Jabba the Hut. It's a "No Fire Zone" where you avoid the wild dangers, risks, and difficulties of being a Christian.

Comfort zones are spiritual prisons that keep you locked up from an intimate, meaningful relationship with God. They are anything that would nudge you to be a slovenly spectator instead of an active participant in God's kingdom. They smother your soul and shrink your heart. Comfort zones put a choke hold on your friendship with God and deafen your ears to hear the sound of his voice. Your comfort zones prevent you from being the dynamic, growing, vibrant person God has designed you to be. They absorb you in a cushy, apathetic, noncommittal, arm's-length relationship from your Creator. Comfort zones keep you lukewarm for Christ. They stifle you from living an extremely radical life for God. Comfort zones are the first signs of spiritual decay. They make you look spiritually beige.

If you've picked up this book, I've got a sneaking suspicion that you want to live an extremely radical life for God. Or at least, you're interested in knowing more about the Christian life. That's why I've filled this book with story after story of young people like yourself: friends of mine who want to be God's person but still struggle like anyone else. You'll find a lot of teenagers in this book just like yourself.

My hope is that you'll discover you're not alone in your struggles and frustrations to be a growing Christian in this crazy, mixed-up world. This book is for people who aren't perfick, er . . . I mean, perfect. It's for young people who struggle with all sorts of different comfort zones but who still have a strong desire to bash away at 'em. This book is loaded with ideas on how to grow closer to God. He's the one who will break the chains of your comfort zones, free you from the sting of sin, and empower you to be more like his son, Jesus.

If you're feeling blah with God or if you're just kicking back in the Jacuzzi of a comfort zone, this book will challenge you to serve others. Serving others in the name of Christ will zap away your comfort zones quicker than anything else. You'll never regret living an extremely radical life for God. By breaking your comfort zones, you'll discover the true, lasting joy of being a child of God.

EXTREME
BEING
FOR GOD

I AM
UNCONDITIONALLY LOVED

Look

Kerry was one of the first girls to come to our youth ministry. She was also one of the first girls to do something extremely radical for God. How? After discovering the wonderful, unconditional love of God, she made a personal commitment to God by surrendering her life to Jesus Christ. Kerry experienced an incredible transformation. She collided with her Creator, and her life has never been the same. What made her decision so radical? Kerry got out of her comfort zone; that safe, warm, cozy place inside all of us that doesn't want to be bothered by anyone or anything. The first step to breaking your comfort zones is being surprised (or reminded) by God's incredible love for you. That's what this book is all about, and that's why Kerry's story is a good place to start.

The first time Kerry came to our Sunday morning high school program, she heard about a week-long mission trip during Easter vacation to Mexicali, Mexico. Not knowing what she was really getting herself into, she signed up. Instead of relaxing at Palm Springs or kicking back at the beach, Kerry spent her week sleeping on the hard, dusty ground; playing with smiling, dirty-faced children; and standing in church services and long food lines with thousands of other high school students. Each day in Mexicali began and ended with a large group meeting of singing, special music, speakers, and small group discussions. It was during one of these meetings that the speaker gave an invitation to those who wanted to make a personal commitment to Christ. It was simple. Nothing flashy. No bolts of lightning zig-zagging down to earth. Kerry simply asked Jesus into her heart. It was her response to God's radical, unconditional love for her.

LISTEN

But God demonstrates his own love for us in this: While we were still sinners, Christ died for us.

Romans 5:8

My hope for you as you read this book is that you discover God's radical love for you. Like Kerry, I hope your life becomes incredibly transformed by allowing God to live in your heart. In order to live for God, you have to be willing to get out of your comfort zones. That means breaking away from

C-O-M-P-L-A-C-E-N-C-Y-A-P-A-T-H-Y-M-E-D-I-O-C-R-I-T-Y-H-Y-P-O-C-R-I-S-Y-A-N-D-S-E-L-F-S-E-R-V-I-N-G-P-A-S-S-I-O-N-L-E-S-S-L-I-V-I-N-G.

It's breaking away from selfishness and the sins that entangle you like a giant, life-squeezing octopus on your heart. The only way to break your comfort zones is by accepting God's love for you. His love frees you to live the wonderful life he has planned for you.

How can you be sure of God's love? Let's break it down in very simple terms. Romans 5:8 says that God demonstrates his love for you in this way: Even though you are a sinner, separated from God because of willful rejection of his ways, his radical love is proved by Christ dying on a cross for you.

God loves you and wants you to experience a life-transforming relationship with him. I've met hundreds of students who have given their lives to God, and like Kerry, their lives have never been the same. For better . . . not for worse. Break your comfort zones today—discover God's 100-percent-guaranteed-unconditional-always-by-your-side-never-leave-you-or-forsake-you-hang-in-there-with-you-4-ever-always-believe-and-hope-in-you-type-of-radical-love-you've-never-seen-like-this-before. (You can take a breath now!)

LEAP

If no one has ever told you about God's radical love for you, here are some more verses to build on understanding how much he really loves you. John 3:16, 1 John 1:9, Romans 3:23, John 10:10. If you haven't given your life to God, take a wild leap into God's love. All you have to do is: Admit your need for him, say you're sorry for your sins, ask him to take control of your life, and begin living for him today. If you've made this decision right now, find someone you can talk to about your new relationship with God. Talk to a friend. Find a church where other Christians can help you grow. Your new life in Christ is an exciting new adventure that'll last a lifetime. If you've already made a decision to follow Jesus Christ, take some time to thank Jesus for his sacrifice for your sins. Ask him to daily fill you with his life and love. Read over these verses. You probably have a "Kerry" in one of your classes just waiting to break her comfort zones for God.

I AM GOD'S FRIEND

Look

In January 1992, our junior high ministry left South Orange County in three white school buses packed with over a hundred screaming junior highers and staff for their annual "Wild Winter Weekend" retreat in the San Bernardino Mountains. Wild Winter Weekend turned into "Wild Winter Wipeout." A bus accident is no way to start a retreat.

Todd and two buses arrived at camp safely, but the third bus missed the turn to camp and continued down the mountain road. A few minutes after Todd arrived, he received a phone call from a highway patrol officer who said that a white school bus had rolled off the mountain cliff in flames. On the bus was Todd's pregnant wife, Tracie, two other staff, and thirty-eight junior high girls. That's all the officer said, except that Todd should get down there pretty darn quick. All Todd could envision was a busload of screaming, burning people flying off a thousand-foot cliff.

Meanwhile, back at the church office, it was just after five and I was about to go home. Two lines rang. Jerry Hill, our executive pastor, picked up one line and I picked up the other. Different sources, same message: "This is Sgt. Jones with the Highway Patrol, and one of your buses went off a cliff. We have multiple injuries, some of them look critical."

As the officer spoke, a major rescue effort was already underway. All the police, ambulance, and search and rescue scanners went off; the story was picked up by every major local and national news station. Within minutes, the phones were buzzing. Panicked moms called in. Dads listening to news on the radio dialed in on their car phones. News stations began to call in:

"This is CNN . . . is it true that your bus went off a . . ."

"Hi! Stan here with the *L.A. Times.* Can I . . ."

"Is my daughter OK? Is she?"

Understandably, parents were very upset. This was the type of major crisis you always hear about happening somewhere in the Ozarks, but we now had to figure out which of the hundred kids was on what bus, field calls from parents and the press, and formulate a crisis plan to handle the situation. Fortunately, we quickly developed a crisis management team, and within a few hours, the immediate crisis was brought under control. Somewhat under control.

After rolling one and a half times off a steep embankment, the bus finally came to a stop on its side. If the bus had rolled off a quarter mile down the road, then it would have careened off a thousand-foot cliff. A couple of people were seriously hurt with back injuries, including Todd's wife. Thankfully, no one was killed. What was a horrible accident could have been an awful tragedy.

LISTEN

My command is this: Love each other as I have loved you. Greater love has no one than this, that he lay down his life for his friends. You are my friends if you do what I command. I no longer call you servants, because a servant does not know his master's business. Instead, I have called you friends, for everything that I learned from my Father I have made known to you.

John 15:12–15

Rolling down a mountainside in a school bus would get anyone out of their comfort zone real quick. This junior high ministry is called F.O.G. (Friends of God). Their purpose is to learn how to develop a better friendship with God. Sometimes it takes something tragic to get our attention, to get us out of our comfort zones, to consider whom our most important friendships are with. When a number of the girls in the accident returned to camp the next day, they were greeted with hugs and kisses from a wild mob of friends. At first news of the accident, a lot of junior highers were wondering if they'd ever see their friends again. Some of them had probably taken their friendships for granted.

Are you a friend of God? Has anyone told you lately that Jesus Christ is the best friend you could ever have? Jesus says that anyone who's willing to follow him is his friend. Are you willing to follow Jesus today? I hope so, because Jesus is the coolest, most loyal friend you could ever want.

Sometimes it's easy to think of God as a really old guy with a long white beard, wearing flowing bed sheets and a Walkman. Other people tend to think God is some type of intelligent, cold, uncaring life force. It is easier to understand who God is when we hear Jesus say, "I have called you friends." As a loyal friend, Jesus laid down his life for you by dying a brutal death on a cross. Why? (1) Because he loves you, and (2) so you could be friends with God forever. Just like any friendship, you prove your loyalty to your friends by doing what they ask you to do (as long as it's completely moral, ethical, legal, and right on . . . not any of that silly, stupid sin stuff). Being a friend of God means doing what he says because he's always looking out for you. Rejecting God's friendship is spiritual suicide because God is the one who offers you eternal life in Jesus Christ. His friendship with you will last forever.

LEAP

Why does it take tragedies or near tragedies to get us out of our comfort zones? What do you tend to take for granted in life? If you were to roll off a mountainside today, are your relationships with your family, friends, and God where you want them to be? What about your friendship with God? What has it been like lately? Take some time to sit down and pray about how you can develop better friendships with God, your friends at school, church, and yes, even your family. Don't let a tragedy catch you in a comfort zone.

I AM A CHILD OF GOD

LOOK

"Despite all my family problems, I know that I am not my family."

Hank and I were sitting in our backyard patio talking about the struggles he had experienced growing up in a broken home. Hank's parents were divorced when he was young, and his mom later remarried. He and his stepdad argued all the time. Their relationship wasn't a pretty picture. As a high school student, Hank had a lousy relationship with his stepdad. At one point, Hank even moved out to a friend's house for a couple of months until their conflicts simmered down.

Now in his early twenties, Hank looks back and realizes that even though he went through so many hard times as a teenager, he is still an important person in the eyes of God. Though his family had problems, Hank understands that he is not the sum total of all his family struggles. That's a healthy attitude. Hank understands that he is an individual created by God: A child of God who is unconditionally loved by his heavenly Father. Hank knows he is responsible for the choices he makes. In our conversation, Hank didn't blame his stepdad or disown his family. He simply admitted that he knows his growing-up years weren't the best, but now, as a young adult, he's responsible for creating his own history. Hank's breaking his comfort zones by breaking free from bitterness and blaming others for his life. Hank knows he's a child of God first. His security and significance rest in his heavenly Father.

LISTEN

How great is the love the Father has lavished on us, that we should be called children of God! And that is what we are!

1 John 3:1

Bitterness and blaming can destroy your spirit. You are not the sum total of your family's problems. Rest in the comfort zone of God's love. The comfort zones of blaming and bitterness are like heavy, rusty chains on your heart and soul.

Is Hank's family situation similar to yours? Since there's a fifty-fifty chance you come from a broken home, 1 John's encouragement to you is that in Jesus Christ you are a child of God. God wants to lavish his love on you. Whether your family is whole, split, separated, blended, chopped, or pureed, God cares about your family. He also cares deeply about the thoughts, fears, and questions you may have about having a family of your own someday. Have you ever said to yourself, "I hate my home life; I'm never going to get married and have kids; I'm not going to screw up my life like my parents did"? A lot of teenagers feel that way. Of course, some teenagers I know use more colorful adjectives and cruder words than I'm allowed to, but the point is clear: Our families have a tremendous impact on our lives.

God can have a tremendous impact on your life if you understand how loved and treasured you are as an important member of his family. He also knows that bitterness is like a nasty poison that chokes your heart and soul. Bitterness will boil deep-seated anger like a smoking, thundering volcano ready to explode molten lava all over the place. God understands how you feel, but he doesn't want you to get burned by bitterness. Being radical for God means growing out of the comfort zone of bitterness. I say "growing" because you can't instantly break every comfort zone you have. Growth takes time. Healing takes time. If you're bitter and angry about your family life, God is the one who can help you grow beyond bitterness. You are not your family. You are a child of God.

LEAP

If you come from a broken family, find or start a group where you can talk about your problems. Don't just hang out with bitter, angry teenagers who use drugs and alcohol to escape from their problems. Face your problems. Talk about your feelings, how to handle conflicts, how to live with a stepparent, how to get along with stepbrothers and sisters, visiting parents on weekends, holidays, your parents' creepy boyfriends or girlfriends, and finances.

I AM CRUCIFIED
WITH CHRIST

Tom and I met in Coco's restaurant to talk about his getting involved in our high school music ministry. His former youth pastor, Eric, was now serving with our youth ministry team and asked Tom to get involved. From the moment I met Tom, I knew he would have a positive influence on teenagers. Plus, he had a very strong recommendation from Eric.

Over Cokes and hamburgers, Tom and I talked about his passion for music. He loved playing the guitar and wanted to use his gifts for the Lord. Eric's youth ministry had a very strong influence on his life, and now, as a college student, Tom wanted to make a difference in the lives of young people. Tom's energy, enthusiasm, and eagerness to lead music for teenagers was contagious. He was ready to start right away.

As always, I began asking a lot of questions. I explained to Tom about our existing music ministry and where I thought he could fit in. I told him that he could begin playing alongside Phil, our current worship leader. I also said that I'd like him to play with Phil for at least a couple of months before he began to lead worship on his own. Tom didn't quite seem to understand.

"You mean I can't lead music by myself?" he questioned me.

My response was something like, "Yes, that's exactly what I mean."

"Why? I can sing. I can play the guitar," Tom said in slight protest.

"Tom, let me ask you a question. When was the last time you led music for sixty people?"

Tom mumbled, "Well . . . I haven't."

LISTEN

I have been crucified with Christ and I no longer live, but Christ lives in me. The life I live in the body, I live by faith in the Son of God, who loved me and gave himself for me.

Galatians 2:20

I explained to Tom why we incorporated new staff members slowly into up-front positions. Phil had years of worship-leading experience and Tom could benefit by learning from him. I also explained that I wasn't ready to hand over an established music ministry to someone with very little worship-leading experience and to someone I, the other staff, and most important of all, the teenagers didn't know at all. Playing guitar and singing was one thing; leading a wide variety of people to experience a significant encounter with God through worship was a lot more difficult than it seemed. Though Tom didn't like what I had to say, he was still willing to be involved and work alongside Phil.

Tom and I have since become very good friends. Over the past five years, he has become a very effective worship leader. Through his love for God and passion for seeing teenagers experience God through worship, he has had a tremendous impact on hundreds of high school and college students. Tom has proven himself to be a capable, faithful servant of

Christ. He is an inspiration to me about what it means to be humble, teachable, and willing to work alongside others.

To become a worship leader, Tom had to die to his idea of what he thought leading worship was all about. He had to die to his expectations about what he wanted to do right away. He had to learn to work together in a team for the good of the whole youth ministry. He had to put his pride to death and trust God that his dream of leading others in worship would be fulfilled. In God's timing, Tom's dream became a powerful reality.

Do you have trouble dying to yourself? Dying to yourself is choosing to live God's way and not your own way. Dying to yourself isn't easy. That's why you need Christ living inside you. Dying to yourself is learning to live a Galatians 2:20 type of lifestyle. It's an attitude that says, "Hey, I no longer live, but Christ lives in me." It's a lifestyle of faith and gratitude toward Jesus who loved you and gave himself for you in his life, death, and resurrection from the dead. In Christ, your old selfish nature has been crucified, and now the new life of Jesus lives inside you. Even though you may struggle with your old nature like Tom did, Jesus inside you can help you to choose to live God's way. Just like he did for Tom.

LEAP

Galatians 2:20 is a great verse to memorize in order to build a strong spiritual foundation for your life. It'll help put things in perspective for you when you're wondering what it really means to be a Christian. Here are some questions to help you understand this important verse a little more:

I have been crucified with Christ.

How has your life been crucified with Christ?

How are you different because of your commitment to Christ?

I no longer live, but Christ lives in me.

What do you think Paul is saying when he says, "I no
longer live"?

In what ways can you tell that Jesus Christ lives in you?

The life I live in the body, I live by faith in the Son of God.

What do you think faith is?

Why is it so important to live by faith in Jesus?

Who loved me and gave himself for me.

How did Jesus prove his love for you?

How can you allow the living Christ to live inside your
life today?

I AM CREATED
FOR A PURPOSE

LOOK

I remember when Ryan was a scrawny little sixth-grader. Heidi, his older sister, was a friend of mine, and whenever I was at their house, skinny, little, blond-headed Ryan was usually sitting in front of the TV watching sci-fi videos. He was a cool kid, but he was still a grommet. (A grommet is a creative term for a junior high surfer kid obsessed with surfing, boogie boarding, girls, and bikinis.) To me, Ryan was simply a grommet, but his sister affectionately called him "Scum." Since they didn't have a dog, Ryan called her "Fido." Scum and Fido. What wonderful terms of endearment!

A few years later, Ryan the Grommet grew into a volleyball-crushing high school student. Since Ryan was now taller, thicker, and wider than me, I wisely no longer called him a grommet. Though Heidi still called him Scum, Ryan was now a stud. Tan, good-looking, and a popular member of his school's volleyball team, Ryan came to our youth ministry a few times, but the powerful pull of partying and chasing girls kept his focus off God. Ryan was a campus god; why would he need God?

It wasn't until a few years later that I asked Heidi how Ryan was doing. Heidi beamed, "He's doing great. He's playing volleyball at Orange Coast Junior College, and he's even going to church again."

"Really?" I asked. "Do you think he'd want to get involved in our high school ministry?"

"I don't know," Heidi replied. "Give him a call."

The next week I phoned Ryan and asked him out to breakfast. Over coffee and French toast, I asked Ryan question after question about what God had been doing in his life.

Ryan described how his high school years were filled with wild times of drinking, doing drugs, and sex.

"But after awhile," he explained, "that lifestyle became so empty. I got so burned out on it."

Ryan went on to explain how he discovered a meaningful relationship with God and how excited he was to be a Christian. In Christ, Ryan found a new purpose for living. That was four years ago.

Since breaking away from the party scene, Ryan became a leader in our high school ministry and has had a powerful influence on hundreds of students' lives. Leading small group Bible studies and teaching teenagers how to play volleyball, surf, and snorkel, Ryan's enthusiasm for God overflows into everything he does. Not only is he still active in youth ministry, he's also in a Christian rock band that plays for youth ministries and in coffee houses. Seeing Ryan break his comfort zones by breaking away from the party scene to be free in Christ has been a tremendous privilege. Through Ryan, God is helping many other students find meaning and purpose for their lives. Ryan has grown from grommet to greatness in Christ.

LISTEN

For it is by grace you have been saved, through faith—and this not from yourselves, it is the gift of God—not by works, so that no one can boast. For we are God's workmanship, created in Christ Jesus to do good works, which God prepared in advance for us to do.

Ephesians 2:8–10

Ryan's band is called "Ninety-Nine." Their mission is the same as Jesus' in Matthew 18—to find the one who is lost. My favorite song of theirs is called "Something Real." It's the story of how Ryan found meaning, purpose, and life in Christ. The chorus to this rocking song comes from Ephesians 2:8–10: "For it's by grace I've been saved and this life is for free, God keeps giving to me. I was created in Christ Jesus for his glory, which God prepared for me."

This song rocks hard for God. It's definitely about "something real" that God has prepared for you. Through faith in Jesus Christ, you can receive the free grace of God. There's nothing you can do on your own to win or earn God's love for you. It's absolutely free and guaranteed to set you free to be the person God has designed you to be.

Ephesians 2:10 also says that you are God's workmanship. Can you believe that? You are a precious work in the process of being created, molded, and shaped by the gentle, loving hands of God. In Jesus Christ, your life has a powerful purpose. God has prepared you for a radical lifestyle of serving others. Some of the most loving, caring people I've met are the ones who have found their purpose in Christ by serving others. That's the person God is designing you to be!

Are you finished yet? Are you perfect? Do you walk on water and remember every Bible verse like a spiritual whiz kid? I hope not because I'd be miserably put to shame. No, you and I aren't finished yet. You know it. I know it. We both know it, but the wonderful thing we also know is that God's free gift of grace empowers us to love him and serve others. Finding peace in Christ provides purpose for your life and direction in how to live it. Just ask a former grommet named Ryan.

Perhaps you find yourself in the same place as Ryan before he broke free from the party scene. You may feel trapped by friends who pressure you to drink or use drugs. Maybe you're held captive by your reputation as a partyer and you don't know how to break away. Worse, if you're addicted to drugs or alcohol, you may not be able to wrench yourself free from what is now a dangerous addiction.

To break away from the comfort zone of partying, try to find someone like Ryan. Someone you can honestly talk to. Someone who's already smashed through the thick wall of abusing drugs and alcohol. Talk to someone who's been where you're at and who can help you get to where they're at today. Ask for their help. Ask God to give you a deeper purpose for your life. Sometimes, the best way to break free is to ask God to give you someone who can help you tear down the wall that's keeping you from something real.

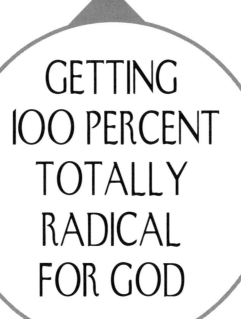

GETTING
100 PERCENT
TOTALLY
RADICAL
FOR GOD

I AM COMPETENT
IN CHRIST

Look

During the one and only summer in college that I was a daycramp, er, daycamp counselor, I witnessed the most violent accident I've ever seen. One day when I was playing with a couple of rambunctious, wisecracking fourth-graders, I saw a small boy standing on the cement about fifteen feet away. He was a cute boy, probably no older than second grade. Innocent. Healthy. Happy. No worries.

Sneaking up behind the cute-innocent-happy-no-worries boy was another little boy his same size. The second boy squatted down behind the first boy, grabbed his ankles and playfully began to pull. Like a slow motion dream when you feel as if you can't react fast enough to save someone, because you're desperately running through oozing oatmeal three feet deep, I saw this terrible tragedy unfold but was too far away to stop it. The smile on my face turned into a look of horror as I whispered under my breath, "No! Don't! You don't know what you're doing!"

After a quick one-two tug, the second boy pulled hard, sweeping the other boy off his feet and into the air. The airborne boy was now parallel to the concrete, gravity rushing to smack him right on his chin.

Finally, the warning leaped out of my mouth, "Nooo!" I screamed, rushing over to try to catch the little boy. Like a falling safe filled with bricks, the boy's chin and head slammed to the hard ground with a sickening thud. The other boy stood up in amazement, a quizzical look on his face wondering, "What's wrong? What did I do?" Dealt a crushing George Foreman blow to the chin, the poor little boy writhed in agony on the ground, not knowing what happened.

Having witnessed a number of split chins suffered by teammates diving for balls during volleyball practice, I clamped my hand on the boy's chin and picked up his little body, screams and all. Blood flowed and oozed through my fingers as I took him to get first aid and call his mother. The ol' "pull your feet out from under you" trick sure did work, but it wasn't funny at all. Who ever invented that one?

LISTEN

Such confidence as this is ours through Christ before God. Not that we are competent in ourselves to claim anything for ourselves, but our competence comes from God.

2 Corinthians 3:4–5

For an unknown, sadistic motive, some adults seem to revel in yanking the feet of young people out from under them. How do some adults do that? By being confidence crushers. Confidence killers. I've seen teachers embarrass students in front of their peers, coaches grab face masks and scream at football players, and parents verbally incinerate their teenage sons and daughters. In the important process of learning to be competent in relationships, athletics, arts, sciences, and other equally important skills, getting your confidence crushed can happen as quick as a seven-year-old pulling your feet out from under you.

One of the most critical tasks in growing up is discovering what you can and can't do. The things you *can* do are called *competencies:* You enjoy doing certain things such as drawing or painting, and you do them well. It means you're competent. Competence develops confidence.

You are competent when you can develop growing friendships. You are competent when you can start and finish certain tasks like homework, chores, or projects. You are competent when you develop certain skills like learning to play different sports, bouncing back from failures, working through a conflict, taking on new challenges, or learning how to fix something. Competence is crucial for your self-image and it ultimately affects how you relate to others. When you become competent at something, then comes the confidence to make a contribution in other people's lives.

I believe every young person has a God-given desire for three important qualities: (1) to be competent, (2) to have confidence, and (3) to be able to make a contribution. Bobby Herron, one of my best friends, described our competence in Christ like this: "In Christ, you are enough . . . he is your competence." I like that.

In God's eyes, you are enough. You don't have to be anything you're not. You don't have to prove yourself to anyone. So what if you can't hit every note you sing or catch every fly ball! You can have confidence in this life because your competence comes from God. If your competence and confidence are rooted in Jesus Christ, you'll be able to make a radical contribution to God's kingdom. You'll discover the wonderful freedom of what it means to be yourself. And you'll never get your feet pulled out from under you by some incompetent moron.

What do you enjoy doing most? What is something you've experienced previous success in? What certain area of your life would you like to develop or work on? What you can and like to do help you discover how unique God made you to be. Following the example in the box below, write down something you're competent in. How does that area of competence develop confidence in you? How can you use your gifts to make a contribution in others' lives?

Competence: I'm good at making friends.

Confidence: Because I can make friends, I can have confidence at my new school.

Contribution: I want to be a friend to someone who doesn't have friends.

I AM HIS SERVANT

LOOK

The tired, frustrated look on Becky's face said it all. If she had wanted to, she could have dug shallow graves for each one of us with her steely-eyed glance. Mercifully, Becky refrained. It was Memorial Day weekend and she had just purchased a ton of drinks, hamburgers, chips, and all sorts of other items for human mass consumption for the beach cookout. The only problem was that nobody told Becky what beach to go to.

Earlier in the week, a decision had been made to go to Capo Beach instead of San Onofre State Beach. On a holiday weekend it was almost impossible to get into San Onofre. Unless you were willing to wait three hours. Unfortunately, nobody adequately communicated that decision to Becky. I tried to call her a couple times. Other people left messages at her home. Whatever happened, the mix-up occurred on my end, and Becky took the hit for us all.

It was an awesome Memorial Day. The searing sun reflected off the churning waves. A cool breeze took the edge off the heat. The water temperature was warm like soothing bathwater. A day at the beach didn't get any better than this. Everyone showed up at Capo Beach around noon. The barbecue was supposed to start around four, but Becky said she would come early with the food so she could spend the day on the beach with everyone else (Yeah right!).

After an hour or so, I began to ask, "Hey, has anyone seen Becky?" Curious looks and shaking heads communicated the same thing: Where's Becky? She's got the food . . . she has to show up!

Unbeknownst to us, while we were lying on the sand, playing game after game of volleyball, and cooling off in the ocean, Becky was getting stir-fried in her sizzling car while waiting in a massive line to get into San Onofre State Beach. Not only did it take her three hours just to enter the parking lot, Becky walked back and forth for an hour on the jam-packed beach looking for us. We weren't even there!

LISTEN

Your attitude should be the same as that of Christ Jesus: Who, being in very nature God, did not consider equality with God something to be grasped, but made himself nothing, taking the very nature of a servant, being made in human likeness.

Philippians 2:5–7

After I profusely apologized to her, Becky forgave me and anyone else remotely responsible for not telling her about the change in plans.

Becky had every reason in the world to stab, skewer, and lay me on a bed of hot baking coals like a stuffed Hawaiian pig. Just shy of stuffing an apple in my mouth, Becky humbly accepted my apology.

Becky is one of the nicest, most selfless and giving people I know. This world needs more people like her. She is what I consider to be a humble servant of Jesus Christ.

Becky doesn't have one of those wild, crazy personalities that draws lots of people around her. She isn't a boisterous stand-up comedienne who makes everyone laugh. Becky is the simple, quiet, friendly girl every group has and that no group can do without. If you're like Becky, I believe God has created you to be a very special person.

Though she is the quietest person on the ministry team, Becky is the most reliable, most loyal team member we have. She has the wonderful spiritual gift of helping others. Without seeking attention for herself, Becky generously gives her time and attention to whoever has a need. You're probably thinking, *What? Is this girl perfect or something?* No, but Becky has chosen to be God's servant as best she can. In his strength.

Somehow, I think Becky has caught the essence of Jesus Christ. When Paul wrote to the Philippians, he tried to help them capture a clear sense of who this Jesus of Nazareth was. Though Jesus was in the very same nature as God, he chose to be a servant. Because of his intense love for this world, Jesus chose to serve humanity instead of staying in heaven. Amazing, isn't it?

Just like Becky, you can let your attitude and actions be like those of Jesus Christ. Without boastful pride, you can say, "I am God's servant." Not many teenagers are willing to say something that radical. You can be different. Jesus wants you to develop your identity in him as a servant. You see, there aren't too many people today who want others to lead them, but almost everyone is willing to have someone serve them. If you want to become great, become a servant. If you want to do something truly remarkable with your life, serve others. If you want to be the most amazing person at your school and in your family, become like Jesus. Be a servant today.

LEAP

Serving others is the surest, quickest way to demolish your comfort zones. Serving others may mean obeying the tug of the Holy Spirit to do that one thing he's been putting on your heart to do. Once you determine that you are God's servant, you cross the line of living for yourself to living for God and others. Take some time out to study these Bible verses on serving others, and discover what a privilege it is to serve the God of the universe. Ask God to specifically show you whom to serve today.

> Whoever serves me must follow me; and where I am, my servant also will be. My Father will honor the one who serves me.
>
> John 12:26

> Am I now trying to win the approval of men, or of God? Or am I trying to please men? If I were still trying to please men, I would not be a servant of Christ.
>
> Galatians 1:10

> Serve wholeheartedly, as if you were serving the Lord, not men.
>
> Ephesians 6:7

I AM GOD'S KID

One of my favorite things about being a daddy is when my little girl, Janae, climbs up on my lap. The big, blue leather reclining chair in our home is "Daddy's chair." Janae and I have more fun in my big blue chair than we would sitting in a two-seater F-16 fighter jet or the front seat of the Colossus rollercoaster at Magic Mountain.

It doesn't matter what time of day it is, but whenever I'm doing my relaxing adult stuff like reading the paper, jotting down new writing ideas, or reading a favorite novel, I've got about 3.8 seconds before Janae vrooms over, yanks my arm, and says, "Stam up, Daddy! Stam up!" Whenever Janae's in her usual "stam up" mood, she either wants to play airplane, go for a short walk to look for our neighbor's cat without a tail, or have me act like a tiger and chase her across the room.

If Janae isn't in a rambunctious "stam up" mood, she runs to her bookshelf, grabs her favorite assortment of literature and pleads, "Read me a story!" Classics like *Where the Wild Things Are, The ABC Animal Book,* and *Ency-*

clopedia Brittanica A–M (she hasn't got past "M" yet . . . she's only four!). She scampers up on my lap and says, "Come on, Daddy, read!" Then, the warmth and softness of Daddy's chair carries both of us into a fantasy world of pictures, dreams, and make-believe. Janae, sitting quietly on my lap, absorbs big words, dramatic gestures, and funny sounds. Before her brown, wonder-filled eyes, stories come alive, and Janae imagines the stories' characters jumping out of the pages to play with her on her daddy's lap.

After reading two to three thousand books, I transform myself into a growling, roaring, tickling tiger and begin to chase her around the furniture on my hands and knees. Janae's squealing, hysterical laughter fills the room. Sitting nearby, cooing and drooling, watching this unusual drama unfold, Janae's six-month-old sister, Ellie, isn't far behind in joining the fun. Playing with two of God's most amazing creations, I'm reminded what a powerful privilege it is to be a daddy. Janae and Ellie are two of the most wonderful blessings I could ever receive.

LISTEN

For you did not receive a spirit that makes you a slave again to fear, but you received the Spirit of sonship. And by him we cry, "Abba, Father."

Romans 8:15

When was the last time you sat in your daddy's lap? No, not your real dad . . . your heavenly dad! You see, the Bible says that God is your heavenly Father and you can approach him like a daddy. You are God's kid. In Jesus Christ, nothing can separate, split, or divorce you from being his kid. Being God's kid doesn't mean you're a silly, immature, seven-year-old brat. You are God's kid in every best sense of the word. God loves to be with you. He loves to read you stories. He loves to put you on his shoulders. God digs you. He's proud of you. He loves the fact that you are his child.

Just as my children are a blessing to Krista and me, you are a blessing to God.

How do you see God? Is he a far-off, vaporous, ethereal being who's part magician, part cosmic cop, and part mean old man? Or is God an aloof, absent-minded professor locked away in his laboratory on some remote planet, not interested in your thoughts, your problems, or your pains? Is God like your vice principal? Your stepdad? A terrifying, black-robed judge sitting high and mighty behind a huge bench? You see, how you view God will determine whether or not you feel comfortable sitting in his lap. I mean, would you really want to get to know someone you're scared of, someone who intimidates you and makes you feel like an insignificant fleck of blush at the bottom of a makeup kit?

Fortunately, God is not like any of our horrible misconceptions. Paul says that because God is your father who loves you, you don't have to be enslaved to fear. You can call him daddy. That's what "Abba" means in Hebrew. Because you've received the Spirit of being a son or daughter of God, you can always cry out, "Dad! Daddy! Father!" and God will always hear you.

Not only does God love you as his child, he also likes you a lot! Have you ever stopped to consider that God likes you? In a world filled with fashion magazines that tell you that you'll never be pretty enough, God says, "You are my child. You are fearfully and wonderfully made." At the gym, where there's so much competition to be thin and have the "perfect" body, God says, "Hey, I like you just the way you are. You're my kid. I've carved you out of the palm of my hand." And in school when you're struggling with learning foreign languages, geometric curves, algebraic equations like F.O.I.L., or you just don't seem to be as good an athlete as the other girls in P.E., God says, "Big deal! So what? I don't care about verbs, A(B + C) (XY & Z), or your fastest mile . . . I care about YOU!"

Knowing how God loves you, likes you, and sees you can radically change how you see yourself. If you feel forgotten or like no one's special kid, then you're in for a big surprise. Be God's kid. The one he loves. Hop on his lap today. He's got plenty of room for you.

LEAP

God loves you because you're his kid. He wants to spend time with you. He doesn't want you to be scared of him. He wants you to sit on his lap and give him all your fears, worries, and concerns. What anxieties or troubles do you need to give God today? Below, write down whatever it is you need to hand over to God today. After doing that, write down what you love about being God's kid.

Lord, these are the things I'm setting in your lap today:

_____

_____

_____

_____

_____

_____

This is what I love about being God's kid:

_____

_____

_____

_____

_____

I AM HIS AMBASSADOR

The country of Haiti is a miserable island set in one of the most beautiful spots on Earth. Perhaps you've heard about Haiti in the news within the past year or two. Haiti is the poorest, most underdeveloped country in the Western hemisphere. It is a deforested land wracked with poverty, malnutrition, corruption, and AIDS, and its history is stained with a succession of cruel and vicious dictators. Haiti is the kind of place most Christians would rather pray for than visit. Except for a friend of mine named Shane.

As a high school student, Shane was deeply involved in our youth ministry's mission and service projects. He regularly ventured to Mexico on our Saturday morning work projects. He also made himself available to help serve in the high school ministry. Whether at school, work, or in another country, Shane has been an ambassador for God. He is what I consider a solid representative, a spokesperson, for Jesus Christ.

When Shane entered college, he began spending his summers as a foreign missionary. For the past two summers,

Shane has visited Haiti as a medical assistant. His grandfather is a doctor, so Shane travels with him to help with medical procedures for the people of Haiti. After working in disease-filled slums and less than adequate medical facilities, Shane came back to America with a new vision for his life. As an ambassador for Christ to the sick and impoverished, Shane's experience in Haiti transformed him.

Leaning on our kitchen counter telling me about his dream to become a medical missionary, Shane's enthusiasm for medical ministry spilled all over our conversation. He left with me recommendation forms for three colleges where he might finish his premed undergraduate studies. It was an honor for me to fill out each form. Shane is an inspiration for every student who wants to be an ambassador for God, whether overseas or here in the United States. His passion for serving and representing God makes his recommendation the kind I love to make.

LISTEN

We are therefore Christ's ambassadors, as though God were making his appeal through us. We implore you on Christ's behalf: Be reconciled to God.

2 Corinthians 5:20

One of your biggest fears in breaking your comfort zones may be wild, scary thoughts like these:

If I totally sell out to be God's ambassador, then he'll probably:

- Send me to a poverty- and AIDS-plagued island like Haiti.
- Make me wear puke-colored, pea-green plaid polyester pants and flammable red polka dot rayon shirts.
- Make me stand up on the lunch tables at school and hysterically scream, "Repent! You brood of vipers!"
- Make me live like a monk and stay celibate the rest of my life. (That means no sex!)

As an ambassador of Christ, the first thing God wants to do is remove any fear you may have about following him. God's not going to pull any funny stuff on you. It's okay to have fears about him sending you where no man or woman has ever gone before, but God would never send you anywhere without first giving you the desire to go there and second, reassuring you with the confidence of knowing that you are right where he wants you to be. Don't allow fear to deep-freeze your trust in God. He has your best interests in mind.

Someday, God might send you to the deep, dark, rhinoceros-beetle-filled jungles of Mufasasimbanala, but you know what? For now, God needs you to be his ambassador right where you are. That means to your family. *Ooohhh, Nnnnoooo!! Don't send me there!* God wants you to be his ambassador to your friends and teammates. Your neighbors on your block. Wherever you are, that's where God needs you to be his representative, his ambassador to a lonely, hurting world.

Shane didn't suddenly wake up from a dream one morning and say, "Haiti . . . that's it! God wants me to go to Haiti!" No, it was over a steady process of faithfully serving others as Christ's ambassador that Shane discovered who God was calling him to be. Then, God placed a desire in Shane's heart about where he wanted Shane to be. Being an ambassador for God begins with being faithful to Jesus today. As you follow Christ, the rest will follow. You may not get to ride in fancy, forty-foot limos with American flags flapping out in front, but hey, you're representing the Creator of the universe.

LEAP

One of the most fantastic ways to break your comfort zones is to allow God to use you as his ambassador. Second Corinthians 5:20 says that God is making his appeal to others through us. Who is God calling you to be his ambassador to today? Do you know someone who needs to be reconciled (restored) to God? What person at home, at school, in your club, on your athletic team, or at work needs the unconditional love and forgiveness of Jesus Christ? How can you be a friend to that person this week? What can you specifically do today to be a positive influence in this person's life for God's kingdom? Close your time alone with God by praying for this special person, and ask God to help you be his ambassador to him or her.

I AM HIS DISCIPLE

If you're wondering how to deepen your relationship with God and discover how to live as his disciple, one essential ingredient for spiritual growth is being involved in a small group ministry. Small groups come in all sorts of varieties, shapes, and sizes: prayer groups, d-groups (discipleship), support groups, sharing groups, drug and alcohol support groups, cell groups. Whatever your youth ministry or church calls it, get in a small group today. The majority of students who have developed a lasting commitment to Christ in our youth ministry have been in a small group.

A small group can help you grow in three ways in your relationship with God: (1) you grow by growing with others, (2) you learn about God's Word and how to apply it to your life, and (3) you share your joys and struggles and pray about the challenges you're facing in your life. When you're in a small group, you soon discover helpful ideas about how to love and live for God in a more meaningful way.

My staff and students have been involved in all sorts of small groups over the years:

- Breakfast Bible studies before school. Students study God's Word and talk about how to be a Christian on campus over pancake syrup and scrambled eggs.
- Twelve-step groups. For students who've come from abusive homes or who have drug and alcohol struggles, this Bible study follows an A. A. format designed to support and encourage young people.
- All girls/all guys groups. These groups have really helped students grow without feeling weird or embarrassed about saying something the opposite sex might laugh or cringe at.
- Lunch Bible studies. These are a great way to take a break from the pressures of school and get a spiritual meal with Christian friends.
- Topical groups. These are groups that usually meet for a short period of time to study a particular topic or popular Christian book.

Whatever the topic or specific design of a small group, small groups that succeed do a few important things: (1) they meet for a specific purpose, (2) they emphasize a high commitment in order to develop relationships and consistency, (3) whatever is said in the group stays in the group. Confidences are kept, not broken, and (4) they are balanced, flexible, and designed to meet the needs of the people in the group. Getting involved in a small group will help you deepen your friendship with God and other teenagers who want to do the same.

LISTEN

A new command I give you: Love one another. As I have loved you, so you must love one another. By this all men will know that you are my disciples, if you love one another.

John 13:34–35

God did not design you to be a Lone Ranger Christian. His design for you is to be his disciple, his follower, by growing and following Christ with others. That's why small groups are so important: They help you think, ask, question, share, pray, and grow with other teenagers who want to grow in their relationship with God.

Jesus had his own small group. He spent three years with his twelve disciples who lived, ate, slept, argued, worked, prayed, learned, and ministered together. Before Jesus died, he told his small group that he would know they were his disciples if they loved one another. Small groups give you the opportunity to know and learn to love other Christians. That doesn't mean that your small group won't have conflict. Jesus played referee plenty of times, but his focus was to help his disciples learn how to love God and one another.

A small group can be one of your best spiritual investments. As Jesus' disciple, surround yourself with friends who want to grow in the same direction.

LEAP

The biggest obstacle that I've seen keep students out of small groups is priorities. "But I don't have enough time . . ." is the most common reason not to be in a small group. With work, school, sports, and clubs, you may not have enough time to be in a small group. That's why I'd encourage you to look at your priorities and make getting involved in a small group a high priority. Your time will follow your priorities. That may mean getting up earlier or cutting something out of your schedule. That's a radical decision to make, but you will never regret getting too radical for God.

CONFIDENCE
CREATORS
TO CRUNCH
COMPLACENCY

I CAN DO ALL THINGS
IN CHRIST

Look

Over the past ten years, I've seen hundreds of students come to faith in Christ. I've also seen a significant number of those same students drift away from God in a matter of a few short weeks or months after making that initial commitment to Christ. What is the difference between a teenager who develops a growing, solid friendship with God and a teenager who dumps God quicker than soggy cereal down the garbage disposal?

One strong reason (there could be zillions) why young people dodge God is an "I can't" attitude. Many students who come to faith in Christ simply get overwhelmed trying to be a Christian. A common misconception I've talked to many students about is the discouraging attitude that makes them feel as if everything depends on them. Forgetting or simply not realizing that it is God working *through* them, their initial enthusiasm turns into tentative commitment. Eager resolve transforms into uneasy hesitation. Commitment turns into complacency. The possible becomes impossible. The loving, tender presence of God now seems cold and distant. Fear replaces faith, and tentative, negative thinking overcomes the dependable promises of God. A distinct change in attitude takes place:

- I can't handle this God stuff.
- I might go to church if I feel like it.
- I try harder and harder, but nothing seems to change.
- I won't ever change, so why even try?
- I've given God my best shot, but enough's enough.
- Maybe I'm just not cut out to be a Christian.

LISTEN

I can do everything through him who gives me strength.

Philippians 4:13

If you're dripping, sweating, pumping, and pushing hard trying to be a Christian, I've got something you need to hear that someone once told me: You're trying too hard!

When Paul was sitting in jail writing this letter to his friends in Philippi, he didn't say, "I can do all things through my own strength." No, Paul said just the opposite. His strength didn't come from himself, but from God, who gave him the strength to handle all things. With God's strength, Paul endured prison, beatings, harassment, storms, slander, setbacks, false accusations, loss of friends, discouragement, and even snakebites. Paul had an "I can" attitude because the source of his strength was God.

If you're sick of trying to be a Christian, it could be because you're trying too hard . . . on your own strength. You're probably not sick of God, but sick of yourself. You only see your weaknesses. You focus on your flaws. You desperately want to change, but when change doesn't immediately come, you're crushed. No wonder you're discouraged!

You want to know the secret of being a Christian? Do everything in God's strength. Not your own. Let the Holy Spirit, God's power in you, change your thinking from "I can't" to "God can." From "I won't" to "God will." Shift your power, your strength, and your effort to the One who has all the power and abundant resources you need to follow him. God would never call you to himself without providing what you need to walk with him.

God's grace in Christ Jesus is his free gift to you and me. Because of his grace, you can stop trying to be a Christian. Because of his grace, you are a Christian. Boom! It's a done deal. You don't make yourself a Christian; God does. You choose to follow Jesus Christ, and the only way to follow him is to rest in his grace, letting him do the work. Nobody said living as a Christian would be easy, but thank God, being a Christian doesn't depend on your strength. My hope for you is that God will lead you not to fade from him, but to faithfully follow Jesus all the days of your life. Though other students may dump God, you can let him be your strength in all things.

LEAP

I hope you've been encouraged by reading this chapter and that you've discovered the secret of living in God's strength. The Bible is filled with accounts of Christians who encountered all sorts of discouragement and setbacks. Here are some verses to show how others used God's strength to follow him one day at a time.

> Praise be to the God and Father of our Lord Jesus Christ, the Father of compassion and the God of all comfort, who comforts us in all our troubles, so that we can comfort those in any trouble with the comfort we ourselves have received from God. For just as the sufferings of Christ flow over into

our lives, so also through Christ our comfort overflows. If we are distressed, it is for your comfort and salvation; if we are comforted, it is for your comfort, which produces in you patient endurance of the same sufferings we suffer.

2 Corinthians 1:3–6

Consider it pure joy, my brothers, whenever you face trials of many kinds, because you know that the testing of your faith develops perseverance. Perseverance must finish its work so that you may be mature and complete, not lacking anything.

James 1:2–4

I have told you these things, so that in me you may have peace. In this world you will have trouble. But take heart! I have overcome the world.

John 16:33

I AM A NEW CREATION

- I feel like driving my car off a cliff.
- I hate myself.
- How could God ever love me?
- I'm ugly.
- I can't seem to do anything right.
- Nobody likes me.
- Why can't I be like others?
- I can't stand my hair.
- My parents pay no attention to me.
- I'm so stupid.
- I'll never change.
- You don't know my problems.
- I'm sick of myself.
- I'd be better off dead. Who would even care?

Comments like these depress me, and after reading them, you're probably depressed too. But these harsh words have names and faces attached to them. They come from students I've spent hours talking with, students who had a completely distorted, yet very real view of themselves. Students who, at one time or another, seriously thought about ending their life. I wish the students who said these things to me realized how God sees them . . . how God thinks of them . . . how he loves them. Perhaps they'd have something different to say about themselves. Perhaps you'll have something different to say about yourself.

LISTEN

Therefore, if anyone is in Christ, he is a new creation; the old has gone, the new has come!

2 Corinthians 5:17

When you become a Christian, a radical transformation that isn't always easy to see takes place deep inside your heart. The first thing to understand about your new relationship with God is that he sees you as a completely different person. You have been reborn. You were once spiritually dead, but now you are alive to God in Christ Jesus. When you look in the mirror, you probably just see the same old you. When God looks at you, he shouts in awe, "Whoa!" In God's eyes, you are a new creation. A new wonder. A masterpiece in the making.

In the crazy, competitive society we live in, seeing yourself as God sees you is hard to do. You are confronted by all sorts of unrealistic ideals and false images that tempt you to constantly compare yourself to them: supermodels, famous athletes, and movie stars. God wants you to see yourself as he sees you. You need not be famous for him to love you. You don't have to be the smartest person in your class for him to like you any more than he already does. When God looks at you, he sees the image of his son, Jesus Christ. When you confess your sin to him, God no longer sees your sin, he sees Jesus. That's what it means to be covered by the blood of the Lamb. Jesus' blood covers all your sin. God sees in you the perfection of his Son. And if that's enough for God, that's enough for you.

Only God can convince you that you are an important, valuable, treasured, new creation of his. If you are struggling with thoughts of suicide or a poor self-esteem, it may take some time to see yourself from God's point of view. To see yourself from God's perspective, you need to allow him to love you for who you are . . . even if that doesn't make sense right now. That's what faith is all about. Faith is saying, "Lord, even though I can't stand myself, I'm going to trust you to change my life. I'm going to start looking at myself from your perspective." As you allow God to love and accept you, you'll warm up to the idea that if God thinks you're someone special, then you really must be! Don't let anyone (even yourself) tell you any different: If you are in Christ, you are a valuable, new creation.

LEAP

All of us have things we don't like about ourselves, but the good news of the gospel is that we are new creations in Christ. A big part of living an extremely radical life for God is viewing yourself as God views you. Staying in the comfort zone of self-hatred is the type of stinking comfort zone God wants to blast through with his love for you.

Take a piece of paper and make two columns. In the left column, write "Old Things." In the right column, write "New Things." Now, in the left column, list the things you don't like about yourself or what you'd like God to change. In the right column, list what you believe God thinks about each area you'd like to change. Are the problems in the left column too big for God? What could be some reasons God is interested in helping you with these areas? How do you think God views your problems differently than you? Are there any steps you need to take to change your self-image?

I AM FEARFULLY AND
WONDERFULLY MADE

LOOK

I usually don't pick up hitchhikers, especially *girl* hitch-hikers.

But I can understand what a drag hitchhiking can be. When I was fifteen years old, I occasionally hitchhiked to work in Laguna Beach. I felt stupid standing on a corner, holding my thumb out, late for work, waiting for a ride. Though hitchhikers can be a weird breed, I'm already weird. I have a special place in my heart for carless individuals.

One day I was driving through my hometown, Dana Point. I stopped at Carl's Jr. for a greasy lunch, and as I left the restaurant, a young teenage girl followed me out. As I was getting into my car, she stopped to ask me if she could have a ride up Pacific Coast Highway. Bewildered by her outright, forward, and unusual request, I sort of mumbled, "Uh, well, yeah . . . sure."

Burning cigarette in hand, she grabbed her knapsack and hopped in my car. Since I didn't make it a regular practice to pick up female hitchhikers, you could say I was a bit flustered. Yes, I was nervous, but on the other hand, I also reasoned that this girl needed a simple ride. No big deal. I'd rather drive her up the road than worry about her being picked up by some psycho, teen-killing predator.

Five minutes into our drive up PCH and after a little bit of talking, the girl turned to me and asked, "Do you think I'm pretty?"

Scary, scary, scary . . . I began to think to myself . . . *Maybe* she *is the psychokiller predator!* I could already see the news flash: "Youth Pastor Becomes Chopped Liver . . . Film at Eleven!"

What was I supposed to say, "No, you're ugly . . . I only pick up ugly hitchhikers!" I sounded like an embarrassed, stammering Elmer Fudd as I said unconvincingly, "Uh . . . yeah. You're pretty." Boy, did I feel stupid.

LISTEN

I praise you because I am fearfully and wonderfully made; your works are wonderful, I know that full well.

Psalm 139:14

Not knowing what to say next, I continued to drive along PCH staring blankly at the road. She said nothing. I said nothing. Resting on the dashboard was my Bible.

"Are you a Christian?" she asked.

Now there was a simple question I could answer without having to think much.

"Yes," I replied. "I became a Christian when I was in high school."

Our conversation didn't go much further than that because we arrived at where she needed to get dropped off. She said thanks and good-bye and was gone.

I drove home perplexed. *That was just too weird,* I thought, shaking my head. What would compel a teenage girl to ask a complete stranger if he thought she was pretty or not? Glancing at my Bible still resting on the dashboard, I thought, *What does it matter what I think? God thinks she's pretty. He created her.* That's something I should have told her! It's too bad I stammered and stuttered like ol' Elmer Fudd trying to catch dat silly wabbit.

If only this teenage girl could have experienced the wonderful security that comes from knowing how special she is in the eyes of God. As a beautiful creation of God, she wouldn't have to question whether or not she is pretty. Her image of herself could be secure in knowing that she is personally and intimately loved by God. She wouldn't have had to ask me, a complete stranger, whether or not I thought she was pretty.

Do you ever wonder whether or not you're pretty? Perhaps you spend a lot of time wondering if girls think you're good-looking. Regardless of what others think, I want to tell you what I didn't tell that teenage hitchhiker. I want you to understand what God thinks about you. You are God's creation. You are a masterpiece in the making. You are made in God's image. Because God made you, you are special! Each one of his creations is a beautiful, precious work of art, and that includes you. If you wonder whether you're beautiful or handsome, pretty or pretty studly, gorgeous or just good-looking, then look in the mirror of God's Word to see your true image. You'll see what he wants you to see. He wants you to reflect the special, unique character of his beauty and strength. That's the type of reflection that will change your life. When you look in God's mirror, you'll see yourself made in his wonderful image. God's mirror never lies.

LEAP

Since God's Word is a mirror to reflect who you are and who he wants you to be, look up these verses. On a sheet of paper, write down "How I see myself" and "How God sees me." Describe how you usually see yourself and how God sees you. Are you seeing the same person that God sees?

> But now, this is what the LORD says—he who created you, O Jacob, he who formed you, O Israel: "Fear not, for I have redeemed you; I have summoned you by name; you are mine."
>
> Isaiah 43:1

> The LORD appeared to us in the past, saying: "I have loved you with an everlasting love; I have drawn you with loving-kindness."
>
> Jeremiah 31:3

> This is love: not that we loved God, but that he loved us and sent his Son as an atoning sacrifice for our sins.
>
> 1 John 4:10

I AM ALIVE TO GOD

In your battle against sin, do you ever feel as if you've been dealt a mean left hook and you're going down for the count? As a Christian, it seems that each day is a new round in the boxing ring. Surrounding you in the packed bleachers witnessing this battle are your family and friends. Some are praying. Some are cheering. Others are laughing, jeering, booing, wondering if this whole "commitment to God" thing of yours is as real as you say it is. They're watching you, questioning if you're going to win or lose. In the far corner is your spiritual opponent, the Prince of Darkness himself: Satan. He's out to prove you wrong. He's out to make creamed Hamburger Helper outta your face. He's got his shiny red gloves on, he's weaving back and forth, shadowboxing, waiting for the bell to ring. What kind of punches will he pull today? When is he going to unleash that lurking left hook of his? What low blow will he try to sneak by you today? In your corner, you're watching him. Waiting. Wondering. Watching his moves.

Man, is he fast, you say to yourself. *And sneaky too.* You just never know what kind of demonic trick he's going to whip out today. Every day, his moves are different. A quick jab here, an unforeseen punch there. All his moves are quick. Subtle. Stealthy. That right roundhouse he pulled on you last week. Boy, did that one catch you off guard. It had been a long time since someone had rung your bell. Almost knocked you off your feet!

Being a Christian isn't as easy as you thought it would be. You didn't realize that Satan would deliver such a constant barrage of colossal one-two combos to your noggin. You get dizzy just thinking about the round you have to fight today. You wonder if you've got the right stuff—the stuff your other Christian friends seem to have—endurance, courage, patience, strength, commitment. The stuff it takes to win the battle for your soul every day.

Looking at your opponent, a torrent of emotions runs through you. Fear. Complacency. Doubt. Intimidation. You think, "Hey, I could settle this thing really fast by just throwing in the towel." You begin to second-guess yourself and second-guess the power of God. DING-DING-DING!!!

LISTEN

In the same way, count yourselves dead to sin but alive to God in Christ Jesus.

Romans 6:11

Too late. The bell's already rung. There's no turning back now. All of a sudden, your coach, Jesus Christ, calls your name and gets your attention. Just the sound of his gentle voice causes all your fears to suddenly vanish. OK, maybe your fears don't vanish in a split second, but at least you know he's with you.

"Okay, here's the game plan for today," he says, looking you straight in the eye. "Same as always, I do the fighting for you and through you. All you got to do is get in the ring. Remember: This battle is mine. It's my power and my strength that you rely on. Satan? He's already lost, but he doesn't realize it. Stick with me; stay close. I'll shield you from his blows. When I move left, you move left. When I jab, you jab. All you've got to do is stay in the ring. That's the tough part, but it's the only way we're gonna win!"

You loosen up your neck from side to side, pop in your mouthguard, make a few quick jabs and begin God's fancy footwork in you. A second before stepping into the ring, you pray a quick prayer, "Lord, how could I have ever thought of throwing in the towel? Sorry about that . . . let's get to work."

Complacency, that ho-hum sensation of feeling like doing nothing with your life for God, is one of Satan's subtle jabs designed to weaken your resolve to follow Jesus Christ. Instead of getting in the ring each day and letting Jesus fight your battle against sin, complacency makes you feel like you're all alone. Complacency causes you to feel like the odds of winning are impossible, so why even try? Complacency is one of Satan's tricks to keep you outside of the ring and inside your comfort zone. He knows that complacency is one of his best blows against teenagers. His temptations come in smooth, comfort-zone-pleasing whispers: *Bible? Why read the Bible when you can watch MTV? You can always read your Bible, but you never know when your favorite music video is going to be on next. A church retreat? But they're not even going skiing! What a rinky-dink youth group you attend . . . You could spend the same amount of money and hit the slopes instead!*

Fortunately, God's Word offers you courage and strength in your battle against complacency. You can deal complacency a devastating blow by counting yourself dead to sin. Instead of lying face-first on the mat, staying down for the count, you can count yourself alive to God through Christ Jesus. Everything you need to walk with God daily is provided for you in Jesus Christ. Endurance. Strength. Power. Righteousness. Courage. Stamina. Perseverance. Grace. Most of all, God's tender love will keep calling you back to himself. His voice will always remind you that you are his child. His voice will remind you that you're alive in him. When you count yourself alive to God in Christ Jesus, here's another thing you can count on: The enemy doesn't stand a chance.

LEAP

In what area of your spiritual life do you tend to become complacent or lazy? What is one area of struggle that Satan keeps jabbing at? Do you feel like you're fighting by yourself? Do you feel like you lack the courage and perseverance to stay in the ring? Why don't you give God that area of your life today? Ask him for the strength to stay committed to him. He has everything you need to walk with him today. Don't allow discouragement, frustration, or your sins of the past to knock you out of the ring. Count yourself dead to sin by counting yourself alive in Christ today.

I AM CONFIDENT IN CHRIST

Look

I know a very special junior high girl named Stacey. Stacey's in eighth grade, and for the past few months, she's become extremely self-conscious. Not unlike a lot of other seventh- and eighth-graders. When Stacey was in grade school, she was a fun, confident, and easy-going girl who laughed at just about anything. Not anymore.

Now, as an eighth-grader, Stacey will barely look me in the eye. I'll ask her how she's doing, and with an unsure half-smile, she'll meekly answer me, "Fine." *Sure.* Stacey doesn't look or sound fine. Do you and Stacey have some things in common?

Stacey constantly thinks about what others think of her. She stays awake all night long worrying about everything she thinks about: *Do my friends like me? Do I have any real friends? Does God like me? Am I a "good enough" Christian? Should I give up all my sports to follow God? Is God angry at me when I sin? Am I pretty? Do boys think I'm pretty? When do other girls have their periods? Does anyone really love me? Am I smart? Am I a good student? What if I don't get all A's? What if I fail a class? What do others think of me? Does anyone else think about as many crazy things as I do?*

In case you couldn't tell yet, Stacey is paralyzed with fear. Just like so many other teenagers in junior and senior high, her whole view of herself is radically changing as she grows older. She is no longer a little kid. I think she sometimes wishes she still was.

LISTEN

Being confident of this, that he who began a good work in you will carry it on to completion until the day of Christ Jesus.

Philippians 1:6

Stacey's once cheerful personality doesn't have the child-like confidence it used to. She is now plagued with fear, doubt, worry, and insecurity. But Stacey isn't alone. Being a teenager today presents lots of ways to get your confidence crushed quicker than you can say, "Cap'n Crunch." Instead of understanding what it means to be confident in Christ, Stacey constantly compares herself to other girls

who are either prettier, thinner, smarter, or better athletes than her. If she's not comparing herself to others, her mind is spinning like an out of control computer hard drive, wondering what others think of her. Fears! Fears! Fears!

If you struggle with fierce, heart-wrenching fears and perplexing questions, then you're like Stacey: You're normal. Everyone wants to be liked. Everyone wants to be loved. Nobody wants to feel, look, be, or act stupid. Your fears and questions are signals that you're growing up. You're facing very real and important issues about how you understand yourself, your relationships to others, and your friendship with God. The real challenge is to not allow your fears and questions to crush your confidence. Especially the confidence you can know and experience in Jesus Christ.

The apostle Paul says that once God starts a good work in you, then he's going to finish the job. He's not going to leave you like a half-finished haircut. Or an uncompleted test. Or a boring, forgotten chore. Or a missed assignment. Or a boyfriend or girlfriend who dumps you for someone else. In Christ, God is going to finish what he's started, and here's the best part of all: God's not finished with you yet! That's a firm promise you can count on and have confidence in when you're feeling like no one cares or understands what you're feeling.

Battling ferocious fears, it's easy to lose your perspective and confidence in Christ. It's easy to forget that Christ wants to give you confidence to crunch your fears. It's easier to freak out on fear than to face it with faith in the power of God. Do yourself a favor; take it easy on yourself. God's not finished with you yet. God's not hard on you like you are on yourself. Do God a favor . . . fling your fears in his direction by putting your confidence in Christ today.

LEAP

Fears can keep you trapped in your comfort zones by paralyzing you from taking action. You don't have to live in fear of your fears. Give your fears to God. One sure way of tackling your fears is by changing the focus of what you fear. The Bible says to fear God, which means to have a radical, awesome, holy respect for who he is. Instead of fearing your fears, live to fear and honor God. Check out these verses that talk about the benefits of living a life that honors God. Fearing God will increase your confidence in him, yourself, and how you relate to others. Write down on a sheet of paper your top three fears and then list the benefits of fearing such a fear (are there any?). Then look at theses verses and list the benefits of fearing God. How can fearing God increase your confidence in Christ?

But be sure to fear the LORD and serve him faithfully with all your heart; consider what great things he has done for you.

1 Samuel 12:24

The LORD is my light and my salvation—whom shall I fear? The LORD is the stronghold of my life—of whom shall I be afraid?

Psalm 27:1

But the eyes of the LORD are on those who fear him, on those whose hope is in his unfailing love.

Psalm 33:18

Teach me your way, O LORD, and I will walk in your truth; give me an undivided heart, that I may fear your name.

Psalm 86:11

As a father has compassion on his children, so the LORD has compassion on those who fear him.

Psalm 103:13

The fear of the LORD leads to life: Then one rests content, untouched by trouble.

Proverbs 19:23

TAKING THE
SHARK BITE
OUT OF
FEAR

FACING YOUR FAILURES

LOOK

Mr. Wilkins, Melissa's high school sociology teacher, started class with a statement and then a question.

"It's a known historical fact that the Christian religion has done more harm to mankind than any other religious group. In fact, Christianity is racist by design. Would anyone like to challenge me on that thought? Are there any Christians in this class?"

Melissa slowly sank back in her desk. She knew how much Mr. Wilkins despised Christians. She felt trapped. Yes, she was active in her youth group. Yes, she was raised in a Christian home. And yes, she was a Christian. But Melissa was also shy. She didn't have what she considered to be a strong, bold faith like her other Christian friends. She didn't like speaking in front of large groups, especially in situations where she'd embarrass herself. And besides, the guy she had a secret crush on sat two seats behind her. At all costs, whatever the question was, Melissa didn't want to be embarrassed. Challenging her faith, Mr. Wilkins only made it worse. "Come on, out of thirty people, there must be one person who's a Christian. Let me see a show of hands."

Melissa froze. She felt like everyone was looking at her. No one else raised their hands. An icy silence fell over the class. Mr. Wilkins changed the subject and moved on. Inside, Melissa slowly started to cry.

LISTEN

As Simon Peter stood warming himself, he was asked, "You are not one of his disciples, are you?" He denied it, saying, "I am not." One of the high priest's servants, a relative of the man whose ear Peter had cut off, challenged him, "Didn't I see you with him in the olive grove?" Again Peter denied it, and at that moment a rooster began to crow.

John 18:25–27

Later that week, Melissa came over to our house in tears. Sitting down with my wife, Krista, she cried as she explained how horrible she felt denying she was a Christian. The guilt and shame she felt was tremendous. Through her tears and frustration she cried, "There are people in that class who know I'm a Christian. I should have said something. What do I care what other people think? I wish I could go back and change everything."

Do you ever feel like you've stabbed God in the back? Do you ever feel like Peter who denied Christ? Has your conscience ever screamed at you, "Traitor! Liar! Hypocrite!" for sitting down when you know you should have taken a stand? In one way or another, we've all turned our backs on Christ and said, "I don't know the man."

Denying Christ happens in a lot of ways: tearing apart your family with cruel words; cheating on a test because you'd rather talk on the phone than study; picking on or gossiping about someone just because they are different than you. It sounds a bit crazy, but every time we sin, we turn our backs on God. We deny we even know him.

Cold, raw fear keeps us from raising our hands when everyone else has got theirs stuck in their pockets. Fear is also the paralyzing force that keeps us from facing failures. Admitting your failures to God is the first step to receiving his forgiveness. Confessing your sin is the bridge that restores your relationship with God. God is in the business of restoring friendships. He doesn't want fear or anything else to separate you from the love he offers in Christ Jesus. OK, you blew it, move on. Do what Melissa did after she let God and herself down. Talk to God . . . get things right. Just like Peter, God still has important plans for you.

LEAP

So you just leapt the wrong way; now's the time to leap back to God and keep living for him. Get two or three close friends, let 'em know what happened, and ask them to pray for you. Walking with God is a whole lot better when you have friends along with you. Remember 1 John 1:9 and ask God to give you the strength to stand for him no matter what anyone else says!

FOCUSING YOUR FEARS

LOOK

"Where's Tiffany!" someone screamed as our six-person raft smashed through a second huge, foaming wall of churning water.

"Don't stop paddling!" Craig, our river guide, yelled back as we blasted our soaking-wet way through the bone-chilling, fear-provoking rapid we had nervously anticipated all day: Satan's Cesspool.

Thankful that its smell didn't live up to its name, Satan's Cesspool is one of the most difficult rapids on the South Fork of the American River. This monster rapid is a Full-Cycle-Deep-Rinse-Scrub-Sucking-Vortex-Maytag-X–1000-Hang-You-Out-to-Dry-Special. It's the heart-stopping, adrenaline-dripping type of rapid that'll rinse out even the most stubborn earwax. The type of rapid you don't want to fall in.

Heading into the rapid, Tiffany, wearing a bright red life jacket, was sitting on the middle right side of the boat directly in front of me. As Craig shouted directions and commands, we plunged down the steep drop and rushed up a steep wall of water banking off a rock.

"Hard right!" Craig screamed.

Paddles dug in. Spraying water eliminated any clear sense of direction. Hoots and hollers shrieked over the thundering rapids. Making a sweeping, banking arc off the pounding wall of water, the left side of the raft went high. The three helpless gravity victims on the lower right side of the raft struggled to hang on. At least two of us did.

Kerplop!

Not realizing the powerful hydrodynamics of whitewater rafting, Tiffany flipped off the right side of the raft quicker than you can say Whirlpool Washer. Ejecting out back first, feet flailing over her head, she looked like a frogman diving off for a reconnaissance mission. Nice technique!

Immediately, we blasted into the second foaming turn, but I didn't see Tiffany break the surface. Was she behind us? In front of us? All of a sudden, in the middle of the second turn, I saw a round lump pop up through the gray rubber bottom of the raft and then disappear. (Remember, we're still battling this carbonated sucker of a rapid.) Again, the lump appeared, making a round impression from underneath the raft's bottom.

Oh no, I thought to myself. *That's Tiffany trying to come up for air!*

LISTEN

But Jesus immediately said to them: "Take courage! It is I. Don't be afraid." "Lord, if it's you," Peter replied, "tell me to come to you on the water." "Come," he said. Then Peter got down out of the boat, walked on the water and came toward Jesus. But when he saw the wind, he was afraid and, beginning to sink, cried out, "Lord, save me!"

Matthew 14:27–30

Peter and the rest of the disciples are white-water rafting on the sea of Galilee. A storm has snuck up on them, brewing a bit of a Satan's Cesspool. In surfing terms, the disciples are getting thrashed. Pounded. Worked. Ready to circle the drain. All of a sudden, through the pounding waves, Jesus appears and tells them not to be afraid. There's no need to fear, he's with them. Peter's so excited to see Jesus that he asks for barefoot surfing lessons. As his toes are getting wet walking to Jesus, Peter pulls a Tiffany maneuver. Seeing the surging waves and salt-spraying wind, Peter flips out and begins to sink.

When have your fears made you take your eyes off Jesus? What has happened in the past week that has caused you to sink instead of stand in your faith?

You can focus your fears, seeing them in God's perspective, when you put your eyes on Jesus. Sometimes that's really hard to do. You can't physically see Jesus. You can't grab his hand and hold on tight. Especially when you're underneath a raft trying to come up for air.

Just like Tiffany bumping her head on the bottom of the raft, fear can make you feel like you're never coming up for air. Fear chokes out faith. It sucks away at faith like the churning waters of Satan's Cesspool. Fear keeps you focused on your difficulties, problems, and circumstances. It does anything it can to keep your attention off Jesus, the very One who wants to ease your fears. Your faith in Christ is like Tiffany's life jacket. When you're under pressure, getting held down by pounding waves, your faith is what helps you break the surface of the water. Faith in Christ gets oxygen to your fear-filled heart. Jesus doesn't promise to take away all your problems and struggles, but he does promise to give you his presence and his peace in the midst of your fears. "Take courage! It is I. Don't be afraid." Go ahead, flush your fears. Focus your eyes on Jesus.

LEAP

Getting a permanent press dunking in Satan's Cesspool is a fear-inducing experience few people look forward to. The same is true if you experience the same types of fears as so many other teenagers: Will I make friends at my new school this year? Will she say yes or no if I ask her out? Will I get beat up after school again? Is my dad going to come home drunk again tonight? Am I pregnant? Do people really like me?

God wants you to live in his peace and not fear. What is a specific fear that keeps you in your comfort zones, the kind that takes your eyes off God? How can you give God your fears today so you can get back in the boat and head toward smoother waters? Sometimes it takes awhile to pry our fingers off our fears. Let Jesus help you with that important process today. He wants you to live in his freedom. Not fear.

P.S. After swallowing 3.5 gallons of the American River, Tiffany finally popped up and was quite thankful for her faith, er . . . life jacket.

TRUSTING GOD IN AN UNEXPECTED PREGNANCY

LOOK

Wendy sat down on a chair in front of all the teenagers in our high school youth ministry. On her knee bounced a chubby, drooling six-month-old baby boy named Kyle. Dressed in a pretty white skirt and pink sweater, Wendy began to explain what it was like to be a new mother. There were dirty diapers to change, clothes to wash, early morning hours to wake up and feed Kyle. As much as Wendy loved Kyle, having a baby was much harder than she expected.

Different teenagers began to ask questions about her pregnancy, Kyle's dad, and how Wendy juggled her many responsibilities. As Kyle gurgled and cooed, Wendy shared her challenges in trying to take care of a new baby. A girl raised her hand and asked, "How do you have time to do your homework?"

Wendy went on to explain how difficult trying to finish high school with a baby was. Wendy was only sixteen years old, and as much as she loves her baby, she wasn't exactly planning on being a mother so young. Wendy and her boyfriend never thought she'd get pregnant.

At the time when their sexual relationship was moving faster than their desire to be teenage parents, having sex didn't seem as risky as it sounded. Wendy had always thought, "What me? Get pregnant? No way!"

A year and a half later, Wendy had a much different perspective on sex, love, babies, and biology. Like thousands of other pregnant teenage girls, Wendy never thought it would happen to her!

LISTEN

"How will this be," Mary asked the angel, "since I am a virgin?"

Luke 1:34

I already know what you're thinking . . . Mary was a virgin. What does that have to do with Wendy and all the other teenage mothers who are clearly no longer virgins? Look at the first part of the verse. Mary asks, "How will this be . . . how could I possibly have a baby?" Mary's just a teenager. She hasn't even graduated from Nazareth High yet. She still lives with her parents. She's never slept with a guy. Never even made out with a guy. The last thing on Mary's mind is getting pregnant and having a baby.

In Mary's day, having a baby before getting married was a strict social and religious no-no. If she got pregnant, she knew her parents would kill her. Whether it's an amazing miracle from God or a horrible mistake made in the heat of the moment, an unexpected pregnancy is an unexpected pregnancy. Mary probably felt as panicked as any teenager would have.

"Yeah right, Mary! God got you pregnant . . . sure! You can stop your joking now, what's his name?"

Who would believe her? What was she supposed to tell her parents? How was she going to explain this one to her fiancé, Joseph?

Trusting God in an unexpected pregnancy requires more faith than the average teenager will ever need. If you're in high school or junior high and find yourself pregnant, God knows exactly what you're feeling. All types of fears, crazy thoughts, and worries run wild through your mind. Facing your family and friends with the news that you're going to have a baby takes tremendous courage. People will give you all sorts of opinions: Give it up for adoption. Abort it. Keep it. Calling "it" an "it" doesn't make your situation any easier. "It" is a baby, a human being, and the baby is *your* baby.

Though Mary was a virgin, she still had to deal with the staggering impact of realizing she was going to have a baby. Yet, she still trusted God. That's my encouragement to you: Trust God in this unexpected pregnancy. If you have a friend who's pregnant, you can encourage her in the same way, too. Trusting God won't take away the difficulty of waking up at three A.M. to nurse or trying to cram for a test with a screaming child, but trusting him can provide you the peace that you otherwise might not have. Trusting God in an unexpected pregnancy like Mary did may just provide you the miracle you need.

LEAP

If you are pregnant or know someone who is, the best and probably the scariest thing to do first is to talk with a concerned adult. Talk with someone who will provide you with the support and resources you need to make it through this difficult time.

If you think you might be pregnant but aren't sure and don't know what to do, look in the yellow pages for a Christian crisis pregnancy counseling center in your town. Christian pregnancy centers can provide you with confidential counseling help, free pregnancy tests, medical exams, and many other helpful services. Your church may even offer free crisis pregnancy counseling services. Even if you're not sure, talking with someone will be an important first step to figuring out what your next step needs to be.

Don't allow yourself to go through this crisis alone. Seek help from Christian professionals who want to help you.

TOTALLY EXPOSED

LOOK

"I can't believe I let him do that to me," Vicki cried to Krista as they sat on the edge of the bed.

"I was so stupid. I really wanted to go out with him, but I didn't want *that* to happen. Now there's nothing I can do to go back and change it all."

We had just arrived at the ski slopes after a ten-hour bus ride for our Utah ski trip. Vicki had pulled my wife aside and asked if she could talk to her. All day long, Vicki had had a miserable trip on the bus. Filled with guilt and remorse, she couldn't stop thinking about what had happened the previous weekend. Krista was the first one she had talked to about what had been bothering her. As they sat inside one of the cabins, Vicki sobbed and explained the events leading up to the night when she lost her virginity.

There was an older guy, a senior on her swimming team, whom Vicki had a crush on. He was tall and good-looking, and though there were dozens of girls who wanted to date him, Vicki was the lucky one who got asked out. Vicki was only a freshman and he was a senior, so that made his offer all the more attractive.

There was nothing incredibly creative about the date. They went out to dinner, did the movie thing, and then parked in some out of the way place. Like any other freshman girl wanting to be liked, it was difficult for Vicki to distinguish the difference between his love and his hormones. One thing led to another, and before she realized what had happened, what she didn't want to happen had happened. Vicki gave away the part of her she could never get back.

Sitting on the edge of the bed with Krista, she now regretted her foolish feelings of infatuation. Vicki wished she wouldn't have given in so easily.

LISTEN

Jesus straightened up and asked her, "Woman, where are they? Has no one condemned you?" "No one, sir," she said. "Then neither do I condemn you," Jesus declared. "Go now and leave your life of sin."

John 8:10–11

Perhaps you can relate to Vicki. There are thousands of teenage guys and girls who have been devastated by the sin of sexual impurity. And I'm not just talking about having sex before marriage. Whether it's wrestling with when and where you can put your hands and on whom, impure thoughts, pornography, late-night cable television, sex-filled romance novels, or fashion magazine sex quizzes, it's difficult to stay sexually pure in a world filled with sexual impurity. You tell your friends you're still a virgin, and they look at you as if you just landed from Jupiter. You tell your friends you're no longer a virgin but are asking God to help you make better sexual decisions, and they think you're a hypocrite. How can you stay pure in a sex-crazed world?

In the story of the woman caught in the act of adultery in John 8, Jesus offers you his perspective on sexual impurity: (1) Jesus doesn't condemn you, and (2) Jesus wants you to make good sexual choices. Never does Jesus say he doesn't want you to experience the wonderful pleasure of sex. (God created it, didn't he?) He wants you to enjoy sex by following his design for a healthy sexual relationship. God's design is marriage and his purpose is for you to be sexually fulfilled by one lifelong partner. Not a string of broken relationships you'll never have use for ever again.

Dragged in front of Jesus and about to be stoned by a group of male accusers (whatever happened to the guy she was sleeping with?), the sobbing woman caught in adultery was naked and exposed for breaking God's law. Jesus didn't condone her sin, but neither did he condemn her. Jesus simply called her to leave her life of sin. That's the same call he has for everyone who struggles with sexual impurity.

If you've made sexual decisions you now regret, you can receive God's unconditional forgiveness by confessing your sin to him. Don't let fear keep you from talking to God about your sexual decisions. He is the one who can give you the strength to make positive sexual choices . . . choices that you'll never regret.

LEAP

One of the best ways of dealing with sexual temptation is having someone to talk to. One of the reasons I encourage teenagers to be in a same sex small group is that a small group is a great place to talk about dating, sexual standards, and how to deal with sexual temptation. Talking with other teenagers who wrestle with the same things you do will give you the perspective you need for your struggle and the support you need to hang in there (see chap. 10). Even though most teenagers can't and/or don't talk to their mom or dad about sex, if you can, that's great. If it's too weird talking to your folks about sex, talk to your youth pastor or an older Christian adult you respect. Talk to someone who will help you develop a deeper respect for honoring God with your body and who will encourage you to make positive sexual decisions. Here are some questions that might also help you think through your sexual choices:

- What kinds of sexual thoughts do you have that are not honoring to God?
- How can certain movies or magazines contribute to sexual struggles?
- What are some healthy alternatives to thinking impure thoughts?
- How can you and the person you date set healthy sexual standards?
- What are the benefits of not being sexually active?
- What are the consequences of being sexually active?
- What is your game plan for waiting to be sexually active until marriage?

FREED BY FORGIVENESS

LOOK

Cindy was one of our key female college staff leaders. As a high school student, she had been very involved in our ministry and talked about the day when she could be a volunteer staff member. Though we usually asked high school graduates to first serve in junior high ministry, we had a strong need for a female staff leader for freshman girls. Cindy was a mature, capable leader who had proven herself time after time in high school, and since she already knew a lot of freshman girls in the ministry, it seemed like a perfect fit.

Cindy's first eight months working with the girls went great. She led Bible studies, met girls for lunch, and went on all sorts of camps and retreats. Cindy's personality was always enthusiastic and warm. She had a very strong and positive influence on the hordes of teenagers who loved her. Then, suddenly, as if a long, silent fuse had been lit long before, Cindy's life exploded in a cloud of guilt and self-hatred. She snapped.

I received a phone call late one night informing me that Cindy had almost driven her car off a cliff. Before all the confusing details had been pieced together, she ran away on a whirlwind tour to visit friends in Colorado and Texas. Cindy's life was now like an unpredictable tornado, an explosive rampage of self-destructive fury.

For as high as the heavens are above the earth, so great is his love for those who fear him; as far as the east is from the west, so far has he removed our transgressions from us.

Psalm 103:11–12

Though Cindy's suicidal thoughts and sudden departure were a complete surprise to my wife and me, we both knew that Cindy's past was far from perfect. Cindy's parents divorced when she was young, and Cindy had been exposed to various forms of abuse. As a teenager, she was traumatized by her past. She interpreted the harm inflicted on her by others as her own fault.

After becoming a Christian in high school, Cindy took the initiative to resolve the pain of her past. She went to counseling, and a number of her most important relationships were restored. As a result, Cindy believed that she was making consistent progress. Always willing to please, Cindy was one of the sweetest girls Krista and I had ever met. Krista and I had spent hours talking with her about her struggles and how she was feeling. It was clear to us that Cindy had the courage to face her problems and a strong desire to help other teenage girls through their own struggles. Krista and I knew that Cindy wrestled with her personal issues, but we severely underestimated the powerful undertow effect Cindy's problems had on her life.

It's been four years and I haven't heard from or seen Cindy. The last time I spoke with her was when she returned from Colorado to get help with her problems. Disregarding numerous letters and repeated phone calls, Cindy avoided all contact with us.

As I look back on that tragic situation and what went wrong, the only explanation that makes sense to me is that the Cindy who thought she was free from her past wasn't really free at all. Cindy was consumed with guilt, *false* guilt, over sins that others inflicted on her. As much as she tried to forgive and forget those who had hurt her, her hideous past kept rearing its ugly face in all sorts of compulsive thought patterns and behaviors. Since Cindy had been open and honest with us about her life, everyone (including Cindy) seemed to think she was making real progress. No matter how free Cindy appeared to be on the outside, she was frozen by the pain of her past on the inside.

My prayer is that you truly experience freedom in Christ from your past. In Christ, God throws your sins away as far as east is from west. He never remembers your sins or holds them against you. If you're tempted to run away from your problems like Cindy, run into the arms of your loving heavenly Father. The one thing he'll never forget is his unconditional love for you. He forgives and forgets all of your sins. That's something to always remember and never forget.

LEAP

What are the nagging sins of your past that keep bugging you? Once you confess those sins to God, how do you think he views your restored relationship? Why do you think God wants you to accept his forgiveness in Christ? Take some time to read Psalm 103:8–12 and answer these questions:

Verse 8: What does this verse tell you about God's character? How does God's character relate to your relationship with him?

Verse 9: What is an accusing, angry person like? Is God like that?

Verse 10: How does God treat our sins?

Verse 11: What is God's love for you like? How does God ask you to respond to his love?

Verse 12: What is the exact mileage of the east from the west? In Christ, how can you forget about your sin just like God has? What have you learned from the story of Cindy?

DISCOVERING COURAGE WHEN YOU FEEL LIKE CRYING

HITTING THE *SWITCHBACKS*

LOOK

My best friend, Dana, had just died. After struggling with cancer for four years, a secondary infection to his brain led him into a coma and finally, to death. His death left a devastating impact on not only his close friends, but on many students in our youth ministry as well. Dana had been a member of our ministry staff for over two years, and he had had a powerful influence in many students' lives. Not only were my wife, Krista, and I trying to deal with our own grief and loss, but we were also trying to help the dozens of teenagers who missed him as well.

It was a few weeks after Dana's death when I received a note in the mail from Chiara Padilla, one of the girls in our youth ministry. Out of all the wonderful, surprising, encouraging notes I've received from students over the years, no other note meant as much to me as Chiara's. Its timing was perfect. I was sad, frustrated, angry, and overwhelmed with the loss of my best friend. Feeling completely discouraged, I lacked the courage I needed to get through this tough time. That's when Chiara's note arrived, and I'm so thankful for how God uses teenagers to minister to youth ministers. Here's the quote Chiara sent:

> There is nothing—no circumstance, no testing that can ever touch me until first of all it has gone past God and past Christ right through to me. It has come that far, it has come with a great purpose, which I may not understand at the moment, but as I refuse to become panicky, as I lift up my eyes to him and accept it as coming from the throne of God for some great purpose of blessing to my own heart, no sorrow will ever disturb me, no trial will ever disarm me, no circumstance will cause me to fret. For I shall rest in the joy of what my Lord is!! That is the rest of victory!!

LISTEN

See to it, brothers, that none of you has a sinful, unbelieving heart that turns away from the living God. But encourage one another daily, as long as it is called Today, so that none of you may be hardened by sin's deceitfulness. We have come to share in Christ if we hold firmly till the end the confidence we had at first.

Hebrews 3:12–14

Getting through Dana's death was like a long uphill climb with a backpack weighted down by grief and heavy feelings of loss. I felt like I was on an endless stretch of steep switchbacks. Switchbacks are the deep zigzag cuts in a mountainside designed to make the ascent easier. If you've ever been backpacking, you know how difficult steep switchbacks are. Switchbacks make an impossible climb possible; difficult, yes, but impossible, no.

Trying to scale difficult problems is like hiking long, steep switchbacks. At times, you just feel like giving up. Your pack is heavy. You wonder when the switchbacks are going to level off. You get tired. Sore. Discouraged. *Why keep climbing if it's going to be so difficult?* you wonder. I've certainly felt that way before. I've climbed switchbacks that were so high and so steep that the altitude and sheer physical exhaustion made me spill my lunch all over the trail. It's at times when you're throwing up and feel like giving in that a healthy dose of encouragement makes all the difference in the world.

Death, difficulties, frustrating sins, and all sorts of other problems can sap your courage before you've realized what's happened. Discouragement can turn you away from God, sending you back down the trail when he wants to see you through it. Hebrews tells us about the importance of encouraging one another. When Chiara encouraged me with the note she sent, she gave me the courage I didn't have. Instead of being hardened with a bitter heart, she helped me to see a bigger perspective of God at work. Just as the writer of Hebrews says, encouragement helps to steady our confidence in Christ. When you hit the switchbacks, grab a friend who'll walk with you along the way. He or she will give you the courage you need to keep pressing on when you feel like turning back.

LEAP

Who helped you through a particularly difficult period in your life? How did that person encourage you? In what specific ways did he or she show you how much they cared about you? Who, in your life, needs to be encouraged? What can you do today to encourage someone else?

STANDING ON THE EDGE

Look

Between guys and girls, it's usually the guys who get blamed for being hormonally hungry and sexually aggressive. Sorry gals, not this time.

Jeremy is a junior in high school, a good-looking, goofy surfer guy. Jeremy's also excited about his faith in God and has made a significant commitment to follow Christ even though his surfer friends think differently. He's been involved in the high school ministry for three years, and by staying plugged into the ministry, Jeremy's developed a lot of friends who encourage one another to take a radical stand for Jesus.

This past summer, after hanging out at the beach all day, Jeremy and a girl/friend (that's girl-SLASH-friend . . . they weren't dating) went to his house to get something to eat. Jeremy and Lisa had some snacks and then sat down to watch television. What Jeremy didn't know was that Lisa liked him and wanted to develop a much closer relationship. What Lisa didn't know was that because of Jeremy's commitment to Christ, Jeremy had set some sexual standards that were different than hers. Lisa was on fire for Jeremy, but Jeremy was on fire for God. As they were watching television and drinking sodas, Lisa hinted in a subtle, nonaggressive way about her true feelings for Jeremy: "Jeremy, would you like to make love to me?"

While most guys would have spewed Pepsi through their nostrils at a question like that, Jeremy jumped all over Lisa with a different approach.

"Whattaya talking about, Lisa? No way . . . we don't need to do that!"

Grabbing his Bible, Jeremy sat down and began sharing with Lisa how a personal relationship with God is far more fulfilling than the temporary pleasures of sex. Lisa, who didn't know God, wanted a very personal relationship with Jeremy. Instead of taking advantage of Lisa's offer, Jeremy took a radical stand for God. By keeping Christ first in his life, Jeremy avoided hurting God, Lisa, and himself by giving in to temptation. That's standing on the edge for Jesus. I'd score Jeremy a perfect "10" for breaking his comfort zones.

LISTEN

The devil led him to Jerusalem and had him stand on the highest point of the temple. "If you are the Son of God," he said, "throw yourself down from here. For it is written: 'He will command his angels concerning you to guard you carefully; they will lift you up in their hands, so that you will not strike your foot against a stone.'" Jesus answered, "It says: 'Do not put the Lord your God to the test.'"

Luke 4:9–13

Lisa's sexual aggressiveness toward Jeremy is the type of thing a lot of teenage guys fantasize about happening to them. If you're a guy wishing you knew someone like Lisa, don't be fooled. Sexual promiscuity doesn't make you more confident, self-assured, and secure in a relationship. More often than not, being sexually active in a dating relationship produces feelings of insecurity, guilt, sexual confusion, and regret once the relationship is over. Students who hop from one sexual relationship to the next never develop the critical skills needed for long-term, stable relationships.

Jeremy isn't perfect, and his decision to take a stand for God doesn't guarantee that he'll always make good sexual decisions. My prayer is that Jeremy will continue to make positive sexual decisions and that God will continue to provide Jeremy the strength he needs to stand for him.

Taking a stand for God means being willing to stand against temptation. In Luke 4, the devil tossed out many tantalizing temptations to throw Jesus off course. On top of the temple, Jesus was faced with taking a stand for God or falling for Satan's tricks. Satan offered Jesus food, pleasure, power, and even safety from a swan dive off the top of the temple. But Jesus knew better . . . the momentary satisfaction of self-centered sin could have eternal consequences.

For forty days and nights, Jesus faced every imaginable temptation, but the Bible only tells us of three. How many other temptations did Jesus have to endure? If you struggle with sexual temptation, then you aren't abnormal or alone. Jesus understands what you're going through and he wants to provide you a way out. If you want to stand firm against sexual temptation or any other sin that's constantly nipping at your heels like an ugly, overgrown rodent (or poodle), here are some ideas that might help: (1) Ask yourself, "What temptations do I struggle with most?" The first step to steering clear of temptation is knowing the type of weeds that grow in your spiritual garden. (2) Avoid temptations that trip you up. Don't put yourself in situations or environments that cause you to stumble. (3) Apply God's Word to temptation. For every temptation Jesus faced, he bonked Satan upside the head with a scriptural 2 by 4 he learned, memorized, and used to stand strong. (4) Ask others for help. You can stay strong by asking a friend to stand with you in your struggle against sin. Christianity is meant to be lived with others, not alone. Though you may face temptations when you're all by yourself, knowing that others are standing with you and praying for you can make all the difference in the world.

LEAP

Take a few minutes to write out a game plan for taking on temptation. Temptation will always try to keep you inside your comfort zones. By God's Spirit, you can send those suckers right back over to Satan's side. When you're done, spend some time praying for God's strength to stand with Jesus.

1. Ask yourself, "What temptations do I struggle with most?"
2. Avoid temptations that trip you up. What kind of situations contribute to crumbling in your faith instead of standing?
3. Apply God's Word to temptation. Engrave these verses on your heart: Proverbs 4:23, 1 Corinthians 10:13, James 1:5, Mark 14:38, Romans 12:21.
4. Ask others for help. Who is someone you can talk to and pray with?

JUMPS, BUMPS, AND THUMPS

LOOK

"Who's going to go first?" we cried, after eyeing a mogul that we thought would make a good ski jump.

"I will!" yelled Dave, as he pushed off with his skis and poles. Dave picked up speed going down the hill, hit the jump, and landed, gliding to a smooth stop.

Trevor, Ian, and I stood a hundred yards ahead of him eagerly anticipating our turn.

"My turn," Trevor hooted, as he initiated his first turn to set up for the jump. Ian and I watched as Trevor pushed and pumped his way down the hill, his ski poles generating more and more speed.

"He's going pretty fast," Ian commented, as we watched Trevor make his final approach to the jump. Almost twenty feet before the jump, Trevor made his last turn, racing toward the smooth launch pad, but as he did, his right ski caught the inside edge. Thrown off balance, Trevor attempted to recover and get his skis in line. (How does the line go? *But to no avail...*)

Now a spinning, exploding wave of snow, Trevor blasted sideways off the jump, his body thrown out of control, his speed, momentum, and weight determining the chaos yet to come. The little girl came first. As a sweet, innocent eight-year-old smoothly snowplowed down the hill, Trevor blindsided her like a ferocious freight train clobbering a helpless Hyundai. After nailing the little girl, Trevor, the screaming snowball of disaster, blasted on and took out her father right at the knees. The accident, on par with ABC's Wide World of Sports's agony of defeat maneuvers, didn't look good. Nobody was getting up.

LISTEN

Humble yourselves before the Lord, and he will lift you up.

James 4:10

The accident scene was a mess. The little girl was screaming, "Daddy! Daddy! Are you okay?" The father

was in agony, holding his knee, struggling to keep from screaming. Ian, who had skied down the hill to get the ski patrol, was now getting chewed out by the man's wife, who had witnessed the whole accident from the ski lodge. Physically unhurt, but with his pride severely wounded, Trevor quietly sat in the snow as the ski patrol took control of the scene.

Admitting fault can be hazardous to your pride. Especially when someone gets hurt and it just so happens to be your fault. Trevor wasn't planning on catching an edge, losing his balance, and becoming a human bowling ball. The strike he scored was a strike against him.

Later, when everyone was down in the ski patrol office, Trevor apologized to the man he'd hit, who was now heading to the hospital. Hanging his head low and apologizing profusely, he tried to explain what had happened. One of the ski patrol men got Trevor's attention, then asked the injured man if he wanted to press charges for the accident. Trevor got a panicked look on his face. Generously, the injured man said, "No, that's okay. If I was his age, I probably would have done the same thing. It takes a man to say you're sorry and own up to making a mistake." Like that, Trevor was off the hook. According to state law, the man could have pressed charges against Trevor for causing the accident. Maybe if Trevor hadn't humbled himself, admitted his mistake, and asked for forgiveness, the man might have thought differently.

Admitting you're wrong, even when it is an accident, takes courage most people don't have. Taking responsibility for your mistakes gives you a shot at receiving forgiveness. Receiving forgiveness and pardon is a whole lot better than getting charges pressed against you. It also prevents selfish pride from taking control of your life. Yes, owning up is a thump against your pride, but it could be the jump you need to get you out of your comfort zone.

LEAP

How has your pride gotten you into trouble? When was a time you were injured or had your feelings hurt by someone, and they wouldn't admit they were wrong? How did that make you feel? Read these verses about pride and humility. Consider how God wants you to break your comfort zones by becoming a person of humility.

When pride comes, then comes disgrace, but with humility comes wisdom.

Proverbs 11:2

Before his downfall a man's heart is proud, but humility comes before honor.

Proverbs 18:12

Do nothing out of selfish ambition or vain conceit, but in humility consider others better than yourselves.

Philippians 2:3

Who is wise and understanding among you? Let him show it by his good life, by deeds done in the humility that comes from wisdom.

James 3:13

Young men, in the same way be submissive to those who are older. All of you, clothe yourselves with humility toward one another, because, "God opposes the proud but gives grace to the humble."

1 Peter 5:5

TOTALLY COMMITTED

Half-hearted, mediocre, lukewarm commitment comes in all shapes, sizes, and spectacular spills. Tentative commitments, especially when sports are involved, produce all sorts of fantastic, flamboyant face plants (falls on one's face).

Waterskiing Wipeouts

Suzanne was learning to cross the boat wake for the first time. We told her to remember to lean back instead of leaning forward. She quickly learned that leaning too far forward thrusts water up the nostrils at speeds in excess of forty miles per hour.

Climbing Crux Moves

A crux move is the most difficult move you make while climbing up a rock. The crux move is the difference between climbing farther or falling as far as gravity takes you. Depending how difficult the crux move, it could mean the difference between life and death. I've seen plenty of students swinging like yo-yos on a climbing rope after learning the critical concept of commitment *after* attempting crux moves.

Trust Fall Takeoffs

Standing on top of a ten-foot-high tree stump, Mark just took too long to jump. The group of students supposed to catch him got bored and stopped paying attention. Mark's initial lack of commitment to lean back and let go led to a severe spinal adjustment when he decided to drop when no one was looking.

Bump Skiing Blowouts

Like snowflakes, no two moguls are alike. They're like chopping up speed bumps and scattering them on a steep hillside.

The trick to skiing moguls is figuring out a line to maneuver through the moguls. The really tricky part is keeping a commitment to staying on that line. Students who haven't skied moguls before soon discover that these kinds of bumps aren't as soft as snow.

LISTEN

Commit to the Lord whatever you do, and your plans will succeed.

Proverbs 16:3

The keys to attempting any extremely radical activity are courage and commitment. In order to consistently break your comfort zones for God, you need to make a total commitment to his work in your life. That's 100 percent unequivocal, completely radical, no-surrender, undeniable, total commitment. Why? Because courage follows commitment.

If you're zipping behind a boat wondering if you should cut the wake, the first thing you need to do is commit yourself to the idea of doing it. Once you decide to go ahead and do it, courage is what applies to your fear of face planting in front of everybody watching. The same is true of following Christ. It takes commitment and courage to follow Christ at school and at home in today's world.

Teenagers I've talked with say, "I could never give up smoking or cussing or doing all the things I like to do . . . it'd be too hard." My response is that if they don't make a commitment to Christ first, they'll never have the courage to change. They also won't have the strength that comes from God to successfully make it through whatever challenge they face. To change takes courage, and courage follows commitment.

God wants your plans to succeed, but first he wants you to make a total commitment to him. Making half-hearted commitments usually results in frustration and failure. This world is filled with broken promises, unsatisfied expectations, and discouraging disappointments. Things like fears, guilt, living in the past, shame, insecurity, and constantly comparing yourself to others are commitment killers that can whittle away your relationship with God.

Whether you're skiing down an extremely steep ski slope, praying for your friends to accept Christ, asking God to help you get through your parents' divorce, or trying to tackle a lousy self-image, commit yourself and your plans to the Lord. Whatever you say or do, commit yourself to his radical design for your life. He will give you the courage to follow through. When you fail, he'll be the one to peel you off the ground from your face plant. Total commitment doesn't mean you'll never fall. Total commitment is discovering the courage found in Christ to stay committed even when you fall.

LEAP

What is the most radical type of commitment you've ever made? What is your all-time worst wipeout? It takes courage to live out your commitments, especially after a severe face plant. Facing your failures is critical to keeping your commitments. Write down one or two discouraging setbacks you've had to deal with in your life. Maybe you didn't make the final cut for a team. You lost a good friend because of a stupid fight you started. You forgot about a major homework assignment and received a poor grade as a result. What did you learn from your setbacks or failures? Did a low level of commitment contribute to the failure in any way? How can God help you to understand the relationship between failure and commitment? In what ways can you deepen your commitment in the important areas of your life? What commitments do you need to put in the Lord's hands today?

INTENSE INTEGRITY

Look

A sure way to stick inside those spiritual growth-smothering comfort zones is to ignore what I call an "integrity check." Integrity checks are those very clear tugs on your conscience about choosing to do right or wrong. They are warning signals you receive from the Holy Spirit right before you make an important decision. Integrity checks and how you listen to them will make or break your character as a Christian. Integrity checks happen all the time:

✔ Since your school is pretty rough, you've thought about joining a gang for some time now. A few of your friends are in gangs, and from the outside, they don't seem so bad. You know that being in a gang will directly conflict with your relationship with God, but what are you supposed to do?

✔ A girlfriend pleads with you to lie for her. She's been dying to go out with this older guy, but her mom won't allow it. All you have to do is let your friend spend the night. She'll say you're both going to the movies, but what are you supposed to do?

✔ The other teenagers you work with are always stealing clothes, purses, and accessories. Your manager finally finds out about it and calls everyone in for a meeting. At the meeting, he says he suspects everyone of stealing and will call the police if the truth isn't told. He's ticked and you know he's serious, but what are you supposed to do?

✓ It's another boring Friday night and the phone finally rings. It's your wild friend Tom with another "great" idea. His dad has a ton of old spray paint cans in the garage that he'll never miss. Tom's already called a bunch of other guys and they're meeting at the park in twenty minutes to graffiti all the playground equipment. Sounds fun, but what are you supposed to do?

LISTEN

> Then Job took a piece of broken pottery and scraped himself with it as he sat among the ashes. His wife said to him, "Are you still holding on to your integrity? Curse God and die!" He replied, "You are talking like a foolish woman. Shall we accept good from God, and not trouble?" In all this, Job did not sin in what he said.
>
> Job 2:8–10

Job had every reason in this world to blow off an integrity check. If you read the story of Job in the Old Testament, you'll be amazed at what God permitted Satan to do to poor old Job. God allowed Job to lose all his megabucks wealth, his sons and daughters were tragically killed in a storm, and then to dump a few sticks of dynamite into the fire, God permitted Satan to afflict Job with oozing, pus-filled sores from head to toe.

As Job sat in a stinking pile of dusty ashes, scraping his wounds with a broken chunk of a Mickey Mouse mug, his wife looked at his pathetic situation and said, "You still trust God? Ha! Why don't you blow off this integrity stuff and just kill yourself? You'd be better off dead than alive. Curse God and die!" For someone in as horrible a shape as Job, that wouldn't seem like too bad of an idea.

Job loses the whole farm. His family. His fortune. His physical health. And then comes the integrity check. His wife challenges him. Will Job curse God for all his terrible circumstances? Will he shake his fist at God and demand an explanation for all of his tremendous losses? What is Job supposed to do?

Instead of blowing God off, Job sticks it to his wife and shows her what real integrity is. Job has discovered that since both good times and difficult times come from God, he doesn't have to let his circumstances run his life. Job chooses not to allow his awful situation to ruin his relationship with God.

In the face of his wife's challenge to curse God and die, Job listens to God and sticks to his integrity.

You may have all kinds of reasons or excuses not to stick to your integrity, but I hope you'll choose to listen to the voice of God and follow his lead in every integrity check you face. But what if you're lonely? Or bored? Or insecure? Or feeling unloved? Or scared? Or intimidated? Even though your emotions can lead you to make poor decisions, you'll never go wrong in choosing to stick to your integrity. Don't allow your feelings to get in the way of following Jesus. Being a person of integrity takes an intense amount of heart-sweating work. However, the pain is definitely worth the gain. Integrity may cost you friends or popularity, but ignoring integrity will always cost you more in the long run. Don't let your circumstances crunch the whisper of the Holy Spirit in the integrity checks he sends your way. Being a person of intense integrity creates intimacy with God and keeps you from getting smothered by your comfort zones.

LEAP

Grab your Bible. Read the first two chapters of Job and discover the intensity of Job's integrity. How do you want your personal character to be like the character of Christ? What kinds of integrity checks do you face most often? If you were invisible and you stood next to a group of people talking about you, what do you think they'd say about your personal character? What kinds of things would you like them to say? What is one practical thing you can do to be a person of intense integrity this week?

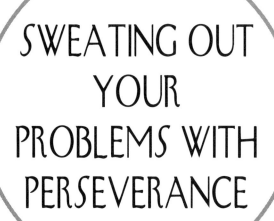

SWEATING OUT
YOUR
PROBLEMS WITH
PERSEVERANCE

I SERVE A GIANT GOD

LOOK

Problems are often like school cafeteria mashed pota-toes: Some students get bigger, lumpier scoops than others. Life has no precise formula for who gets served what or how much. As you well know, every teenager has problems, but why is it that some teenagers get giant, industrial strength problems? Take some of my friends for example:

Jennifer's dad has beaten and sexually molested both her and her sisters for years. The county social services knows about the problems but does nothing. Because of her dad's abuse, Jennifer uses drugs and alcohol to cauterize her feel-ings of shame and hatred. Last I heard, Jennifer was home-less. Every so often, Jennifer comes around asking for help, but she always ends up running away again.

On one of our rock-climbing trips to Joshua Tree Na-tional Park, Tom showed up out of nowhere. He hadn't signed up for the trip, but after an intense argument with his dad, he drove out to the desert to find us. When Tom and I went for a walk to talk about what happened, Tom began screaming at the top of his lungs about how much he hated his dad. And I mean screaming! For Tom's dad, good was never good enough. Straight A's weren't enough. Neither were high SAT scores and advanced placement classes. His dad kept pushing, pushing, pushing. And Tom kept screaming. I finally grabbed Tom in my arms and hugged him as he slowly began to calm down and weep like a little child.

LISTEN

David said to the Philistine, "You come against me with sword and spear and javelin, but I come against you in the name of the LORD Almighty, the God of the armies of Israel. . . ."

1 Samuel 17:45

As a teenager, David was served megablockbuster-size problems in the form of a huge, ugly, nine-foot-tall, God-cursing giant named Goliath. Every wimp, I mean, warrior in Israel was afraid to fight Goliath. Not only was Goliath twice as big as everyone else, he also had the latest in Philistine battleware: Giant sword. Giant spear. Giant javelin. Giant squirt gun. David had a stupid little sling and five rocks. Not exactly high-tech smart weapons. But, David warned Goliath: "I've got something you don't got, Mr. Fathead Philistine . . . I'm coming against you in the name of the Lord Almighty." That night in Israel's camp cafeteria, David served up Goliath's head with mashed potatoes and assorted garnishings. David's attitude about tackling giant-size problems offers hope for the struggles you face each day.

First, David's attitude was, "Hey, I serve a giant God." David didn't concentrate on the giant in front of him, he focused on his God who promised to go before him in battle. God wants you to understand that as you turn your struggles over to him, he'll go before you in your battles.

Second, David ran toward his problem. He didn't run away from Goliath. *Why would David do such a stupid thing?* you wonder. David ran closer to Goliath so he could take better aim at his target. If David had run away from Goliath, do you think Goliath would have stopped his pursuit? No way! He was going to kill this little Israeli gnat who teased and taunted him in front of all his troops. If David had run away, he would have taken a flying javelin right in the back. When you run away from your problems, they keep chasing you down like Goliath. Problems don't go away. Like a speeding spear, problems pursue their target until they hit their mark. The only way to tackle your problems is to chase them down.

Third, David fought in the Lord's strength and not his own. Before taking on Goliath, David said, "All those gathered here will know that it is not by sword or spear that the Lord saves; for the battle is the Lord's." David fought in the name of the Lord, and it is from God that he received his strength. On his own power, there's no way David could have pounded Goliath into the ground. By fighting with God's help, David discovered a powerful source of strength and courage. In the Lord, David had everything he needed. David's battle attitude can teach you how to take on troubles that are tearing you to shreds. David said, "I serve a giant God." In God's strength, you can say the same thing, too.

LEAP

Are you taking on your problems in your own strength or God's? Do you tend to focus on your problems or focus on the giant God who wants to go before you in your battles? Do you run away from your problems or toward them? What problem are you dealing with this week that you need the strength of a giant God to help you conquer? Turn your struggles over to God today by acknowledging that his strength is sufficient to handle anything you give to

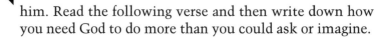

him. Read the following verse and then write down how you need God to do more than you could ask or imagine.

> Now to him who is able to do immeasurably more than all we ask or imagine, according to his power that is at work within us, to him be glory in the church and in Christ Jesus throughout all generations, for ever and ever! Amen.
>
> Ephesians 3:20–21

Lord, this week I need you to be a giant God in my life by

_____

_____

_____

_____

_____

_____

_____

WITH MY GOD, I CAN
*S*CALE A WALL

LOOK

"Hey, Todd and Rich! Are you guys freezing as much as I am?" I chattered through my wind-chilled lips and icy teeth.

"Yeah," came a short, cold reply.

Heat conservation. End of conversation.

It was 2:00 A.M., pitch black (except for our cosmic canopy of twinkling stars), and colder than a walk-in meat locker in the Arctic Circle. Sitting at nine hundred feet above the forest on Tahquitz Rock, Todd, our junior high pastor; Rich, a high school student; and I, the fearful leader were stuck on a tiny ledge tied to a little tree. Like the one you see in cartoons. What had started earlier as a fun day of rock climbing the thousand-foot face of Tahquitz, ended up being a Disney story of epic adventure. A freezing epic adventure.

Wearing only T-shirts and shorts, Todd, Rich, and I got on the rock later than planned. In our first hour, we somehow got off route. In normal language, that means we were lost. We searched for over an hour looking for the right crack lines to ascend. Climbing with two ropes instead of one, we were slower than pudding dripping down a dry rock. All day long, our climb was a laborious puzzle of playing vertical Connect the Dot on our intended route. By 7:30 P.M., the sun was saying "sayonara" in the west. I was leading.

Todd screamed up to me, "Joey, climb faster! It's getting dark!"

Oh really? I put my cappuccino maker, Tom Clancy novel, hairbrush, and mirror back in my knapsack and kept climbing. We were still three hundred feet from the top. Climbing by braille was not my favorite way of spending a Saturday evening.

At 8:30 P.M., I climbed over a tear-inducing, lip-quivering, treacherous, eight-foot-high "Hail Mary" headwall (a large, overhanging obstacle), found the tiny tree Wile E. Coyote always hangs on to, tied in my rope, and then belayed Todd and Rick up the route.

The climb was supposed to take three and a half hours. We completed it the next morning in just under twenty-four. Now we had to face going home. We were in deep yogurt and we knew it. All our families knew was that we had gone rock climbing for the day, and we hadn't returned by dark. (What's wrong with this picture?) Even though we returned home alive, the three of us knew we were dead. Dead meat. Our welcome-home party was a lynch mob.

LISTEN

With my God I can scale a wall.

Psalm 18:29

What are the large walls you're facing in your life right now? What are the seemingly insurmountable barriers you're scared to climb alone? What kinds of dangers and risks are keeping you from moving forward, away from your fears?

When I reached the eight-foot headwall on Tahquitz, I was scared to the point of whimpering and tears. *How am I going to get over this thing*, I wondered. My last piece of protection was twenty feet below me. If I fell, I'd fall a total of forty feet before the protection caught me. That's forty feet of playing human bowling ball I wasn't willing to curl up for. Crouching at the base of the headwall, my fingers cramming into a small horizontal crack, my feet slipping, I flipped through my rack of gear searching for the right-size piece to put in the crack. Finally finding one, it didn't fit very well. Meager protection is better than no protection. Hammering up and down like a speedy sewing machine needle, my feet were slowly losing the gravity battle. Quiet prayers of desperation, last rites, and funerals ran through my mind.

"God, you've got to get me outta here . . . Help!"

The next moment I looked at the top of the headwall above me, and encircling a blinking star was the faint outline of a round, iron piton (a piece of climbing protection equipment usually placed in cracks) nailed into a crack. Nothing more than a God-given gift of hope. Grabbing a couple carabiners (oval-shaped climbing gear used for attaching ropes and equipment), I lunged toward the piton and frantically clipped in. I kinda wish all my prayers were answered that fast!

You may be looking at the problems in your life like a huge headwall looming in front of you. You wonder the same thing I did, "How am I going to get over this thing?" Just like the star shining through the iron piton, Psalm 18:29 provides a bright burst of hope for you. With God, you can scale a wall. God promises that if you hang on to him, he won't let you fall. With God, you can scale any problem you have. Will everything turn out fine? Maybe.

Maybe not. Will persevering through your problems be easy? Probably not. The most important thing God promises during your struggles and problems is his presence. With God in your life, you have an incredible source of strength, power, guidance, and direction. He will provide you with the perseverance you need to climb over your problems. He'll place pitons where you least expect them.

LEAP

What kinds of headwalls are you facing right now in your life? What problems do you need God's strength to persevere in? Take a sheet of paper and draw a line down the center. At the top left column, write "My Walls." At the top right column, write "God's Perspective." After you've listed the walls you're facing on the left column, write down what you think is God's perspective of your problem in the right column. Write down how you believe he would want you to handle the problem. Include ideas about talking to someone, creating an action step to take, or an attitude you want to work on. First Peter 5:7 says, "Cast all your anxiety on him because he cares for you." God wants to provide you with pitons for your problems. Give him your cares and worries today!

SHAKING IT OUT

LOOK

Getting thrown into the pool for the third week in a row was getting old. And painful. It was our Sunday evening Bible study and now that it was summer, we met at Krista's mom's house because it had a pool and Jacuzzi. Chicken fights. Marco polo. Splashing wars. Flips. Wild dives. And wipeouts.

Our students loved hopping into the pool during those long, hot summer nights after Bible study. Amidst hoots, hollers, and laughter, they also loved seeing me get thrown into the pool with my clothes on. Ha-ha. Real funny.

Glen, one of my best buddies and burly volunteer staff leaders, and Peter, a hefty high school senior wrestler, had hunted me down the two previous weeks and baptized me with a full immersion dunking against my will. Since I was a lot weaker than these two behemoths, I didn't even attempt to put up a fight. Why put up a fight when I was going to be the only one who got hurt?

Krista's mom's pool had an upper and lower deck. The upper deck was about four feet above the water, and it was from this deck that Glen and Peter decided to launch me once again. With Glen holding my hands and Peter my legs, they picked me up like a sack of cement and began their heave-ho count. The only problem was that these two gorillas didn't know how to count. ("Duh, do I let go on 'three' or after we say 'three,' which in swing time is really three and a half?") So, with little grace, care, or technique, they launched me.

"One . . . Two . . . *THUMMP! Splash!*"

Somewhere between two and three, Peter and Glen hurled me into the air. Up, but not out. Airborne for approximately 1.3 seconds, I came straight back down, smashing my right hip and rear end onto the hard, wood deck.

"Oooohh," came the laughing cries of dozens of onlooking teenagers.

Like a crumpled dead body thrown overboard, I crashlanded into my watery grave with a horrific body flop. By the time I came to the surface, my right hip felt like it had been pushed through to my left hip. Moans, ooohs, aahhs, and screams of hysterical laughter demonstrated emotions of pity and pleasure at Peter and Glen's botched toss. Me? I wasn't laughing. In the next two seconds, the psychokiller look on my face quickly silenced anyone who was.

LISTEN

Therefore, since we are surrounded by such a great cloud of witnesses, let us throw off everything that hinders and the sin that so easily entangles, and let us run with perseverance the race marked out for us. Let us fix our eyes on Jesus, the author and perfecter of our faith, who for the joy set before him endured the cross, scorning its shame, and sat down at the right hand of the throne of God.

Hebrews 12:1–2

What was I supposed to do? Burning with pain, my hip quickly informed my brain to verbally dissect Peter and

Glen. I wanted to kill . . . okay, that's too extreme . . . let's just say "torture" them. But what was I really supposed to do? I was surrounded by a crowd of teenagers who knew I was hurt and angry. Everyone had just witnessed my receiving a severe dose of youth pastor abuse. It was one of those rare moments when teenagers get to see their youth pastor in raw, animalistic pain and curiously, eagerly wonder, "What's he going to do? What's he really made of? Is he going to beat 'em up?"

If it wasn't for God's grace and a thousand angels surrounding Peter and Glen, I would have ripped their fingernails out one by one. I was in physical pain, my pride was wounded, and I was embarrassed for being drop-kicked into the pool. Grimacing and restraining my tongue from lashing out, it was all I could do to keep my words and actions in check. With a growl, I limped away like a wounded animal.

What do you do when you're hurt, embarrassed, or angry? How do you respond when you're surrounded by friends who wonder what your next move will be? I can truly understand if your gut reaction is to want to destroy anything within a fifty-foot radius, but God's Word offers a better alternative. Instead of getting tangled in sin, the writer of Hebrews says to shake out that temptation by fixing your eyes on Jesus. Rather than crucify the clown who just pegged you, get your eyes off the pain and run with perseverance toward the author and perfecter of your faith.

The reason why the Bible says to fix your eyes on Jesus is because when Jesus went to the cross, he intentionally broke every one of his physical, emotional, and spiritual comfort zones. Everything he did leading up to the cross went against his natural human reaction to lash out and fight for survival.

Jesus wants to help you trade your natural reactions for supernatural responses. When you're tempted to fight back or scream when someone hurts you, fix your eyes on Jesus. As someone well-acquainted with pain and suffering, he understands how you feel. He will help you shake out the temptation to shred the other person to pieces. That's good for you . . . and lucky for them.

LEAP

What is your personal game plan for responding to pain-filled emergency situations? How do you react when someone hurts your feelings? How would you advise a friend to handle a disagreement or fight with another friend? Thinking about how to handle situations before they happen and get out of control can help you fight your natural reactions with supernatural responses. Instead of fighting, fix your eyes on Jesus by knowing how you want to handle conflicts before they occur. Write down three to five specific ways you will try to control your words and actions when you feel like ripping someone apart limb from limb.

DISCOVERING THE WONDERFUL, HILARIOUS JOY OF GOD

Look

Mark was a small freshman with glasses who wasn't afraid to laugh at himself. With all your finest imagination, enjoy his most embarrassing moment.

In between classes, Mark had to hurry to his locker to grab a couple of books. As all lower species *(freshman punkicitus)* on the predatory high school food chain, Mark was given a bottom locker to share with another freshman. In order to see inside of it, he practically had to lie down on his stomach to dig through the piled assortment of books, papers, rotten food, and leaking pens.

On this day in particular, Mark was hunched over, squatting on his knees while an older, female, senior life-form hovered over him, grabbing her books from her locker. Her locker was four lockers above Mark's. Approximately two lockers below her locker was the opening of her big, baggy sweatshirt. Mark's small head . . . her big sweater . . . you're beginning to get the picture.

Hearing the bell ring, books in hand, Mark leapt to his feet and stood straight up inside her sweatshirt. A flailing, spinning life-form inside her sweatshirt, the screaming senior stepped back, trying to shake out her sweatshirt's contents. Covered with a soft cotton material, Mark stumbled, his glasses twisting off his head, wondering who had wrapped this thing over his head. Neither of them knew what had just happened. This one-headed, four-legged, mass of mutated confusion finally separated, each person flustered and wondering how many people had just witnessed the "sweatshirt surprise." Mark and the senior girl looked at each other, shared a faint, embarrassed smile, a quick shrug, and then zipped off to class. I wonder if they ever met in the same way again?

LISTEN

Consider it pure joy, my brothers, whenever you face trials of many kinds, because you know that the testing of your faith develops perseverance. Perseverance must finish its work so that you may be mature and complete, not lacking anything.

James 1:2–4

There's nothing like the wonderful, hilarious joy of God to break your comfort zones. Mark's embarrassing moment and his willingness to share it with others is the type of personal freedom and laughter this world needs more of. Too many teenagers are afraid to laugh at themselves because they think they won't look cool. Others are scared people will think they look stupid. So what! Who cares? Go ahead and laugh! When you're old and gray someday, lying on your deathbed, you won't look back and wish that you could have been "cooler." You won't say to yourself, "If only I could have kept a straighter face. I wish I would have been more serious."

In God's eyes, laughter is serious business. Young people who know how to laugh are serious about the reality of God's unquenchable joy. Even in your problems, the Bible says to consider it "pure joy" when your faith is tested.

Perseverance is a character quality you can't do without as a Christian. Perseverance keeps you hanging in there when you feel like hanging up your faith. Laughter is a wonderful way to stop taking yourself and others so seriously. Joy is the result of knowing that God uses your difficulties for a specific and meaningful purpose.

Does that mean you're supposed to laugh when someone dies? Are you supposed to laugh at world hunger, disease, war, and poverty? Of course not! James says to consider it pure joy when your faith is growing and developing because of the challenges you face. The end result is maturity, wholeness, completion, and a strong sense of not lacking anything you need in this life.

Being able to laugh at adversity because of knowing how God uses challenges to carve our character is a mark of a maturing Christian. God knows that maturity isn't a stuffy, constrictive, serious, and proper set of appropriate attitudes and behavior. Maturity is recognizing God's design for spiritual growth and allowing his Spirit to carry it out in your life. God's design for spiritual growth includes loads of laughter, spontaneous joy, and hysterical notions of freely receiving his grace to accept and enjoy each day as a free gift from him. Go ahead and laugh! Just watch out for baggy sweatshirts!

LEAP

What is your most embarrassing moment? Would you describe yourself as a laughing, joy-filled Christian or a sober, serious Christian with a stiff outlook on life? How can you get more serious about God's joy in your life? What makes it hard for you to laugh at yourself? What difficulties keep you from experiencing God's joy? How can God use your struggles to develop perseverance in your faith? Though you may find it difficult to laugh about your problems, how can you discover God's joy in spite of your circumstances?

BOASTING
IN YOUR BLUNDERS

LOOK

"If I can't be good and perfect all the time, then I'd rather not even try to be a Christian at all," Kim blurted out. She was extremely frustrated with her relationship with God.

"Wait a minute," I responded. "Who said you had to be perfect? Are any of us perfect? Are you and I ever going to stop making mistakes?"

Hanging her head low, Kim mumbled, "Well . . . no."

Kim had hit a low point I think every teenager hits in their faith at one time or another. She was struggling with temptation, her view of herself, and her perspective on God. Kim thought that really good Christians didn't struggle with sin and temptation. Her fixed, static view of God was that, "Once I give my life to God, my struggles and problems will go away. God will take care of everything." Kim was consumed with guilt because she wasn't the person she thought God demanded her to be. A lot of her friends partied and their lives were fine. Partying looked fun to Kim, but she knew it was wrong. "If I'm a Christian, why am I wanting to do the things I know I shouldn't do?" From her perspective, Kim thought she shouldn't even be having these tempting thoughts and struggles. This was not fun. Kim definitely was not experiencing the big yellow happy-face, joy-filled

Christian life. Her whole view of herself and her faith was turned upside down like a big frown.

LISTEN

But he said to me, "My grace is sufficient for you, for my power is made perfect in weakness." Therefore I will boast all the more gladly about my weaknesses, so that Christ's power may rest on me. That is why, for Christ's sake, I delight in weaknesses, in insults, in hardships, in persecutions, in difficulties. For when I am weak, then I am strong.

2 Corinthians 12:9–10

After explaining how confused she felt about her faith, Kim went on to describe her stormy relationship with her mom. Not only was Kim expected to get straight A's, her mom was extremely demanding in all areas of her life. Kim felt like she was constantly performing for her mom. When she did something well, Kim received her mom's approval. When Kim failed or didn't do "as good as she could," then her mom made her feel awful. Is it any wonder that Kim viewed God like she did her mom? *If I'm a really good Christian, then God will love me. If I'm not good, then God won't love me? Right?*

Wrong. God does not love Kim or you or me any more or any less depending on whether we are good or bad. God's love is unconditional. That means regardless of the condition or situation you find yourself in, God still loves you. Because Kim viewed God like she viewed her mom, Kim fell into the trap of performance Christianity. She was trying to get God's approval by what she did or didn't do. Kim hadn't discovered what it means to be weak in Christ.

Paul, a big, important church leader, was struggling with temptation, a huge sucker of a thorn stuck right in his flesh. He begged God to take it away. He wanted to be strong. Free from temptation. Good. Perfect. Like Kim, he thought he shouldn't have to deal with this temptation stuff anymore.

But God had a different plan and he still does. What he said to Paul is the same thing he wants to say to Kim. It's also the same thing he wants to say to you: "My grace is sufficient for you, for my power is made perfect in weakness."

To a group of rugged, individualistic Americans who want to be strong and in control, it seems ridiculous to be strong in your weakness. God wants you to rest in his grace and his unconditional love and acceptance of you. Christianity isn't about jumping through flaming hoops like circus tigers. Following God is finding your sufficiency, acceptance, and freedom in the cross of Jesus Christ. You don't do the work; Jesus already did. You'll still struggle with different temptations at times, but in your weakness, you can rest in the power of God. That's why Paul said, "If that's the case, great! Let me tell you about all these other weaknesses so Christ's power may rest on me." Sounds strange to boast in your blunders, huh?

That's because you serve a wonderful, mighty, loving God who loves to give away strength to his children. Remember: You serve God. Not a demanding mom.

LEAP

Believing you have to perform for God to win his love and acceptance is a form of trying to control your walk with God. Why is that true? It keeps you in the center of your life instead of with God, because your performance rests on you. Staying in the performance trap is a major comfort zone that constantly snaps back! It did for Kim, and it will for you. It's hard to admit weakness, but God wants to free you from having to perform for him. What is God calling you to let go of today? How can you pry your fingers loose of the struggles you're holding onto too tightly? In what ways can God's strength change your perspective on your weakness? Write down your thoughts on the statement "When I am weak, then I am strong." How can you put those words into practice in your life today?

TAKING A
STAND
AT THE COST
OF GETTING
BURNED

FIRING UP FOR GOD

LOOK

One thing all little boys have in common is their passionate love for matches. However, good little boys obey their parents (and Smoky Bear) and don't play with matches. Bad boys, like me, play with matches and are called "pyros." In my family, I've always been called "Pyro Joe" because of the time I almost A-C-C-I-D-E-N-T-A-L-L-Y burned down the whole house.

One hot, smoggy, August Saturday, I was bored and decided to get a little adventurous with my incendiary skills. I grabbed three blue matchbooks, a couple of waxed paper sandwich bags, and my beach bucket full of water . . . just in case. Our front hedge was about seventy-five feet long and six feet high, dividing our yard from the neighbors' yard next door. Hanging over the front hedge was a huge, fifty-foot-high, wide-spanning magnolia tree.

My parents were gone for the weekend. My five sisters and little brother (and our elderly baby-sitter) were inside the house while I knelt on the other side of the hedge with my matches and sandwich bags. The dry, brown hedge was as crisp as a desert tumbleweed. I stuffed two bags into the hedge as starter fuel. I lit a single blue match. Wanting a little more kick to the flame, I then ignited the whole matchbook. As it sizzled to life, I threw the burning matchbook onto the bags in the hedge. Bad mistake.

At first, the flames slowly licked the sandwich bags. Then the small fire began to grow. Whoosh! All of a sudden, the hedge crackled and popped, the flames igniting the tinder-dry leaves and branches. My small innocent match fire instantly grew to the size of a hearty campfire and quickly began to devour the hedge. Now it was time to play firefighter instead of firestarter, but I only had my stupid little bucket. Little did I realize that what I really needed was a fire hose.

Grabbing my water bucket, I splashed the hungry leaping flames in a futile attempt to extinguish the raging inferno. The twisting, dancing flames evolved into an angry, devouring, consuming wall of fire. The hedge was now what firefighters appropriately call "fully involved." I ran full speed around the hedge to the water faucet by our front door and desperately twisted the nozzle on. In surreal slow motion, the water swirled, inching up to fill the bucket. Taking a frantic look back at the hedge, I saw ten-foot-high flames now roaring to the tips of the overhanging branches of the magnolia tree. Like the raging fire, fear and adrenaline swept through every pulsating vein in my little, terrified body. The fire was out of control. The whole world seemed to be on fire, and I didn't know what to do. Jettisoning my bucket, I dashed around to the side of the house, hopped the fence into our backyard, and hoped for a miracle.

LISTEN

Shadrach, Meshach and Abednego replied to the king, "O Nebuchadnezzar, we do not need to defend ourselves before you in this matter. If we are thrown into the blazing furnace, the God we serve is able to save us from it, and he will rescue us from your hand, O king. But even if he does not, we want you to know, O king, that we will not serve your gods or worship the image of gold you have set up."

Daniel 3:16–18

I got fried by my folks for lighting that fire. Fortunately, before the flames ignited the whole magnolia tree and our house, our next-door neighbor grabbed his garden hose and doused the burning hedge.

In the Old Testament, three young men faced a particularly different type of fire fight. While I ran away from my fire in fear of getting caught, Shadrach, Meshach, and Abednego actually walked into a blazing furnace for refusing to worship a golden idol. They were caught standing up for God. Don't you just love how they taunted their nemesis, King Nebby, "But even if he does not (save us), we want you to know, O king, that we will not serve your gods or worship the image of gold you have set up"? Shadrach, Meshach, and Abednego were so fired up about their faith, so consumed with their love for God, that they were totally willing to be torched. That's what I call being on fire for God!

When you take a stand for Jesus Christ at the cost of getting burned by those who ridicule you, you show the world how firm your faith really is. You prove to God where your true allegiance lies. Being fired up for God means refusing to bow down to the modern idols in our society. It's amazing how we create idols out of the things God provided simply for us to enjoy:

- Materialism: worshipping and craving the latest nifty stuff
- Love: searching for the "right" person to meet our every need
- Money: wanting and loving money for money's sake

- Fitness: sweating out our hearts for a perfectly sculptured body
- Music: worshipping rock idols

Ever since Adam and Eve bit that rotten apple, human beings have worshipped things that they can see, smell, taste, touch, and hear instead of honoring and worshipping the only true God. In themselves, there's nothing wrong with material goods, love, money, fitness, music, or any other thing. But, when you give things first priority in your life over God, then that one "thing" has now become your idol. The sad irony of it all is that you serve *it.* Your idol doesn't serve you. Idols never serve their subjects.

The one sure way of staying fired up for God is to develop a daily passion for Jesus Christ. Loving God before anything else will keep you clear of bowing down to man-made idols. When you're fired up for God, you'll be able to blaze through your comfort zones like sizzling waxed paper. You'll light this world on fire for God.

LEAP

Write down three ways you want to be fired up for God. How can you accomplish these three ways to develop a closer walk with God? What are the possible obstacles you might face along the way? Who can help you ignite your love for God? Pray to serve God and only God today.

_____

_____

_____

_____

_____

_____

_____

STICKS AND STONES CAN BREAK YOUR BONES

LOOK

Whew! I was finally going to get some quiet time alone with myself and God. It was midway through a week-long mission trip to Mexico, and after the first few long, tiring days, I found a precious twenty minutes in the morning to steal away to spend time with God. Quiet. Peaceful. Relaxing time alone before another busy, hectic day.

Positioning my beach chair along a dirty, ugly, green-scum-filled swamp (there weren't too many places to hide from three thousand people), I sat down and closed my eyes. *Aah! This is great,* I thought to myself. *Just me and the Lord. Alone. No interruptions.* So I thought.

A few minutes later, I noticed a teenage guy sitting in the dirt about fifty feet away from me. Unlike most teenage guys, this one was crying. Bawling really hard. My immediate reaction was, *Ignore him. He's not in my youth group. I don't even know him. This is my time. I don't even see him.*

I opened my Bible and began to read. *Ho-hum, dee-dee-dee. Isn't this quiet time great? Just me and the Lord,* I thought again to myself. Floating my way, more sobs and sniffles reminded me of the boy's bothersome presence. Just me and the Lord. And that crying kid!

How was I supposed to ignore him? I wanted to, but I knew God was tugging on my heart, saying, "Come on, Joey! Get off your duff!"

Okay, okay, Lord. I'm going, I'm going.

The guy's name was Chris, and he had just blown it. Blown it big time. He had just done something really stupid and now really regretted it. When I asked him what was wrong, he explained that his motives for coming on the mission trip were all wrong. There was this girl in his youth group that he really liked. He thought she liked him too, but when they arrived in Mexico, it was obvious that she liked some other guy. A bigger, more handsome guy. The kind of guy Chris was not, but Chris still thought that he could impress her.

While standing in the food line, Chris and his competition got in an argument in front of the girl. Chris said something stupid to the big guy, then smacked the big guy's bowl of cereal out of his hands. Dumb move. Not wise. Cheerios and milk everywhere. The girl was not impressed.

"That was a stupid thing to do!" she fumed at Chris. "Why don't you just get out of here!"

LISTEN

When words are many, sin is not absent, but he who holds his tongue is wise.

Proverbs 10:19

Chris quickly discovered how words have a peculiar way of boomeranging back to wound the one who launched them. Throwing words around carelessly got Chris in trouble. He found out the hard way that words can really hurt. Especially from the girl he liked. I wonder if Chris would have rather taken a rock to his head instead of getting yelled at and embarrassed by the girl he was trying so hard to impress?

If you desire to grow in your relationship with Christ by taking a stand for him in any and every situation, holding your tongue will show others how serious you are about following God's wisdom. When you hold your tongue instead of hurling a burning boomerang designed to blast someone else, you take a clear stand for God.

Sin has a sneaky way of getting into what we say. You've seen it happen many times before: A group of your friends gets together and someone pulls out a juicy piece of gossip about a certain person at school. Before you know it, everyone is chewing, gnawing, and devouring every tidbit as if it were a tender, succulent steak. Like wolves at the kill, it's a feeding frenzy. You're wondering what to do? It's so easy to talk about other people! But all it usually takes to finish this flesh-eating feast is for one person to take a stand and say, "Hey, wait a minute. This is getting out of control . . . why don't we talk about something else? I wouldn't want a bunch of people shredding me to pieces like raw meat!"

So how did Chris untangle himself from the sticky web he had woven with his words? He and I spent some time talking about how he handled the situation and what he needed to do next. Even though he had blown it, he knew that he could at least try to repair the damage he had done. Now was the time to say something right. Something hard to say. Something like, "I'm sorry. Will you forgive me?" Chris and I ended our conversation by praying together. I asked God to give Chris the courage to take a stand for Jesus by apologizing to his friends. When we finished praying, Chris looked at me and said, "Ya know, when I was crying and saw you sitting over there, I prayed that you would come over to talk to me. You looked like someone I could talk to, and I'm really glad you got out of your seat to talk with me. Thanks." Does God work in strange, wild ways or what?

LEAP

Have your words gotten you into trouble lately? Maybe you've been the victim of gossip and you're tempted to start a few rumors to get back at the people who hurt you? Before you start speaking with a forked tongue, flip open your Bible and see what James has to say about the strongest muscle in the human body. Read James 3:2–13 to find out God's plan for how he wants you to use your tongue. God is ready and willing to help you hold your tongue.

NEVER TOO YOUNG
TO STAND

I can't stand most high school graduation ceremonies. First of all, the silly clothes are downright dangerous. According to recent statistics, flammable parachute clothing burned 382,631 students during the 1995 commencement exercises. The pointed cardboard hats, which nobody knows which way to point when they put them on, resulted in over 17,161 eye injuries in East Coast schools alone. Some students don't even live to see themselves graduate!

Second, most high school students would never even think to join a gospel choir. If school officials are going to make seniors spend money on renting the choir robe outfit, they should require all freshmen students to sign up for Gospel Music 101. Then, all the students would have four years to practice gospel music so they could perform at their own graduation ceremony. And another thing . . . sometimes they're called graduation exercises, but have you ever seen anyone actually exercise at a graduation? Now let's talk about graduation speeches.

I've never understood why the "smartest" people in school say the dumbest things during graduation speeches. The guy or girl speaking, usually dressed in a white choir robe (intellectual purity?), speaks on behalf of the entire graduating class. If I spoke as a representative of my class, I'd be really careful what I said. I'd try to say something different than the typical graduation speech, which goes something like this:

We are the leaders of the future. *(Oh really, who says?)*
We are the hope of tomorrow. *(When?)*
We will change the world. *(Change what?)*
We will one day make a difference. *(How?)*
We are the architects of the twenty-first century. *(But who will fix my plumbing?)*

Leaders. Agents of change. Difference makers. The great hope of tomorrow. In the future. Mañana. Somehow. Somewhere. Sometime. Someday. Ho hum . . . when are they going to throw their hats? That's really the best part about this graduation stuff.

LISTEN

"Ah, Sovereign LORD," I said, "I do not know how to speak; I am only a child." But the LORD said to me, "Do not say, 'I am only a child.' You must go to everyone I send you to and say whatever I command you."

Jeremiah 1:6–7

Graduation speeches are a lot like political speeches. They sound good and seem really attractive, but months (days? minutes?) later they're forgotten. Someday we'll make a difference. We'll be the leaders of the future; not now, but in the future. When we really grow up, that's when we'll change the world.

Someday is no day. God is looking for young men and women who will live to carry out his life-transforming,

world-changing kingdom work *today*. Not someday. Not no day. Not tomorrow. Not in the future, but today. God wants to use you today to transform the world. There is no higher calling you could have than to bring God's radical message of unconditional love through Jesus Christ to this dark and desperate world. People who live by graduation promises quickly become disillusioned old people who wonder, *What is the use in trying to change the world?*

You're thinking, *Me? Why would God want to use me? What could I possibly offer him?* Just take a look at the life of a young man—yes, a teenager—named Jeremiah. God called Jeremiah to bring his message of hope and renewal to the people of Israel. Israel had turned its back on God, and Jeremiah was God's number one choice to round up God's scattered flock. In Jeremiah's own eyes, he was just a teenager. *How could God possibly use me?* he wondered. *I'm just a kid!* In God's eyes, Jeremiah was a special, uniquely appointed prophet with a divine purpose. God said, "Don't say you're just a teenager. I have chosen you. I'm the one sending you. I will protect you. Lead you. Guide you. I will put my words in your mouth. Don't be afraid . . . I'm using you and I'm taking care of everything else!" Wow!

Like Jeremiah, you are a special, unique teenager to God. He wants to show you how significant a life of service can be to the people of this world whom he cares about. Do you want to be God's tool for transforming people's lives today? Do you want to see his purposes carried out in your friends' and families' lives? Do you want to live an authentic, Spirit-filled life of following Christ today? Then break your comfort zones by allowing God to use you to make a radical difference in this world today. You are never too young to take a stand for Jesus. That's something you can do today. Not someday.

LEAP

How is God calling you to take a stand for him today? What kinds of negative and defeating attitudes keep you wondering if God can use you as a positive influence in others' lives? What are you most passionate about as a Christian? How can you use your gifts and passions to serve others? What friends of yours are willing to pray to see your campus transformed by Christ?

What comfort zone do you need to leap out of today to live for God? What is one simple, practical way you can be an instrument of God today?

HERE I AM, LORD!

One of the most inspiring persons in my life during the past year has been a guy by the name of Mike Maciborski. While his tongue-twisting last name makes him sound like a Russian wrestler—I'll buy you lunch if you even dare to pronounce it correctly—Mike has actively served in the college ministry at our church for the past two years. Just recently, he took over the leadership of the whole ministry. The comfort-zone-breaking leap Mike took to make that move is a great story in how God works through daring young people totally sold out to him.

Just out of college, Mike was aggressively recruited by a couple of different companies. Since both companies wanted Mike, each one offered competitive salaries with long-term income growth potential. Mike chose ADP, a large, nationwide company, and began life in the fast-paced corporate world.

During his first year with ADP, Mike was getting very involved in our college ministry. Mike is one of those guys

I always like to hang around with. He's always positive, never has a bad word to say about anyone, and his enthusiasm for life spills all over everyone he meets. A natural leader and friendly person, Mike justly earned himself the nickname "The President" from everyone else on the college ministry team. As an organizer, Mike could rally people to get involved with events, to sign up for trips, and to carry out the details people like me usually forget. Mike's unique personality and spiritual gifts quickly made an important contribution to the college ministry team. Mike soon found his friendships and ministry to college-age people to be one of the greatest sources of spiritual and personal fulfillment. The only problem was that his job required so much of his time and energy.

Divided between work and the college ministry, Mike began to seriously pray about entering the ministry. He sensed God putting a strong desire in his heart to go to Bible school to learn more about his Word and ministry. That began a series of long conversations between Mike and me about the direction of his life.

LISTEN

Then I heard the voice of the Lord saying, "Whom shall I send? And who will go for us?" And I said, "Here am I. Send me!"

Isaiah 6:8

After a lot of prayer and at least a dozen cups of coffee from all of our one-on-one talks, Mike finally made the courageous decision to leave the security of a good job at ADP. Mike went from a well-paid position to a no-pay position as a college ministry intern. He also decided to enter Bible school full-time to prepare himself for ministry service. Serving people for God's kingdom ultimately became more important to Mike than anything else. That is a radical step. That's what I call faith. That's what we need more of!

When God called Isaiah to be his prophet to the nation of Israel, it wasn't like Isaiah interviewed for the position. God didn't even aggressively recruit him. God said, "Whom shall I send?" He was asking for anybody, any warm body, anyone who would listen to his call.

Isaiah's response is the same response God is looking for from you today. God is looking for young men and women who are ready to break their comfort zones for him. He's looking for people like Mike who unashamedly say, "Yo! Lord! Over here! Yeah, yeah! That's right, send me!"

God wants young people who are sold out to being sent out.

What does it take to reach the point when you're ready to step out for God like Mike did? First, begin by doing some of the things Mike did. The simplest place to start is to pray about what God wants you to do with your life. It doesn't matter if you're a seventh-grader or a freshman in college. Start now by asking God what kind of person he wants you to be and what he wants you to do for his kingdom. Second, talk to older Christian people whom you know and respect. Find someone who will listen to your ideas and will give you wise counsel about your future. Often, God uses important role models and mentors in our decision making. Third, continue to walk daily with Jesus. A growing relationship with Jesus will develop in you a deeper sense of God's work in your life. Allow the Holy Spirit to move and direct your decisions in ways that please God and that produce the fruit of the Holy Spirit in your life (see Galatians 5). As you pray, seek solid, godly advice, and pursue a deeper relationship with Christ, God promises to show you where he's sending you.

LEAP

No, you don't have to wait until you're out of college with a high-paying job to break your comfort zones for God.

God wants you to grow where you're planted today. There are plenty of places he wants to send you today. It may be into the garage to help your dad clean it. It might be across the street to visit a sick neighbor. Maybe just cleaning the kitchen with a good attitude is the only thing God's concerned about for you today. You probably won't pack your bags today for Africa, Bosnia, or China, but that's not completely out of the picture . . . I know a number of students who've gone halfway across the world on foreign mission trips. The most important thing is to begin with a willing heart to be sent and used by God. The next step is to find a ministry of service where you can begin to serve people as God wants you to. Practice these two things and you are off to a great start in breaking your comfort zones for our awesome God.

OPPOSING FORCES

LOOK

You may be reading this book really wanting to break your comfort zones for God and live for him in the most radical way possible, but part of you is saying, "Yeah, I want to be a Christian, but you don't understand my situation. You don't know what I'm up against!" For teenagers like yourself, being a Christian can be a daily battleground with friends and family who don't understand your decision to follow Christ. If you're battling opposing forces in your faith, then the good news of this chapter is that you're not alone. Let me introduce you to two of my friends whose situations you might be able to relate to.

Don made a commitment to Christ when he was a sophomore in high school, but it wasn't the type of commitment his parents were very excited about. Don's mom is an alcoholic, and his dad is a busy executive who's hardly ever home. Whenever Don tries to bring up spiritual matters, he's quickly ridiculed and criticized for being a religious fanatic. Don feels like a stranger in his own home.

Emma wasn't raised in a Christian home. In fact, her family's religion is very different from Christianity. Her parents aren't very happy about her attending another youth group. "What's wrong with our church?" they accusingly ask Emma as if she was attacking her parents' way of worshipping God. "The youth group at your church is dead," Emma responds. "The students at your church aren't interested in growing closer to God and no one ever comes." Back and forth, Emma and her parents argue about God, and like always, the argument ends up with yelling and tears.

LISTEN

But I tell you: Love your enemies and pray for those who persecute you, that you may be sons of your Father in heaven. He causes his sun to rise on the evil and the good, and sends rain on the righteous and the unrighteous.

Matthew 5:44–45

Choosing good friends. Making right decisions. Not giving in to peer pressure. Being honest. Fighting sexual temptation. Keeping your cool. Holding your tongue. Living as a Christian is hard enough without facing opposition from the people closest to you. In your daily battle to live God's way and not the world's way, the last thing you need is someone getting in your face and saying Christianity is a waste of your time. You know it's not, but what are you supposed to say to the person criticizing you? Maybe it's best to follow Jesus' advice: Say nothing and pray for those who persecute you.

When Jesus told his followers to love and pray for those who made fun of God, he offered his disciples a powerful weapon against the opposing spiritual forces. Jesus understood that the opposing forces aren't people and their words. The real enemy is Satan and his demonic forces.

Jesus told his friends, "Listen, even though these people persecute you, our heavenly Father still loves them. We need to pray that God will change their hearts."

If God wanted to, he could destroy the unrighteous. He could swipe away every person who mocked his name like a bothersome gnat. The fact that God allows the sun to rise each day on the evil and the good is proof that he wants to redeem this lost, broken world through his Son, Jesus Christ. He wants every person to come to faith in Christ. By praying for those who persecute you, you authentically demonstrate God's love to those who need it most. By loving your enemies you are accomplishing something far more important than anything you could ever say. Loving and praying for your enemies shows that your life has truly been transformed by God. And when you know you've been transformed by God, there's really nothing more to argue about!

LEAP

Loving and praying for those who persecute you sounds nice, but it's actually pretty hard to do . . . especially when you feel like ripping the other person's head off. Praying for people who get in your face and make fun of Jesus Christ will definitely bump you out of your comfort zones. If you're facing opposing forces, ask for the Holy Spirit to give you his strength to not get into meaningless arguments or yelling matches. Ask for the wisdom to respond in a loving way. Though your natural urge may be to want to defend God, ask for help to love the other person into God's kingdom. God's a big boy, he can defend himself. He needs you to be his child who shows others what a transformed life is really all about.

FIERCE
FRIENDSHIPS

TAKING SOME
GOOD ADVICE

LOOK

Thirteen years later, I still wish Bob would have taken my advice. It wasn't the best advice. It wasn't the worst advice. But like most advice, it was good advice. I believe it could have saved Bob from a lot of harm. It could have saved his relationship with God.

It was my senior year of high school, and I had just become a Christian a year earlier. A lot of friends I used to party with were thinking it was some sort of "religious phase." Since I had been the ringleader for a lot of wild parties, everyone was waiting to see how quickly I'd return to my old ways.

For me, I was excited about Jesus. I knew there was no turning back. My friends didn't understand how empty and meaningless I felt after four years of drinking and doing drugs. Almost overnight, my life had been radically transformed by the living God. In Jesus Christ, I had purpose, satisfaction, and a true reason to live.

Bob was one of my buddies on the volleyball team, and I really looked up to him for his commitment to Christ. He had become a Christian when he was in junior high, and I learned a lot about God from his example. We had spent a lot of time together. Bob was one of my closest Christian friends. Sadly, our friendship slowly began to change.

Bob had begun dating another friend of ours named Lisa. Lisa was a nice girl. Attractive. Funny. The only problem was that Lisa liked to party. In fact, before I became a Christian, Lisa and I had been to lots of parties together. Since she was neither a Christian nor very interested in becoming one, I had a talk with Bob about not letting a dating relationship get in the way of his most important relationship. Bob's response?

"Oh, I know. We're just dating a little. I know what you're talking about . . . I'll be careful."

That was the last conversation I had with Bob about girls and God.

LISTEN

See to it, brothers, that none of you has a sinful, unbelieving heart that turns away from the living God. But encourage one another daily, as long as it is called Today, so that none of you may be hardened by sin's deceitfulness.

Hebrews 3:12–13

If you see a friend heading off in the wrong direction in their relationship with God and take the comfort-zone-breaking risk of talking to them, then my hat goes off to you. You are a true friend!

As brothers and sisters in Christ, we're told to help one another by making sure none of us are deceived by the power of sin. Too often, we forget that sin has a deadly way of blinding us to our own weaknesses. A little compromise here, a little compromise there! By following the herd, we've become a rump roast, and Satan is laughing all the way back to the barn. That's why you and I need Christian friends who have the courage to tell us the truth about our lives, even if we don't want to hear it.

Giving and taking good advice is hard to do. It's difficult to hear, but it just may save you or a friend from ship-wrecking your relationship with God on the sharp rocks of sin's deceitfulness. What keeps you from telling your friends the good advice they need to hear? The truth about their lives that they need to hear? Is it the fear of rejection? Is it not wanting to make waves in your friendship? Is it conflict you want to avoid? Are you afraid of being called self-righteous or judgmental? Telling your friends the honest truth about their dumb decisions is a sensitive, difficult thing to do, but it's a clear sign of a true friend. You'll never have to say to yourself, "I wish I would have said something earlier." If you've been making decisions lately that you know don't please God, my prayer and hope for you is that you have a friend who will help you get back on track. Even if you don't, you can ask Jesus Christ, the best friend you could ever have, and he'll give you all the help you need. I've seen too many students trash their walk with God for the garbage of this world. Why trade the rich, golden promises of God for stinking garbage in the gutter? I tried talking with Bob, but his heart grew hard. Is your heart growing cold like Bob's?

My prayer for you is that you don't become another Bob statistic. God is waiting to receive you back into his arms with love and forgiveness. All you need to do is repent of your sin and give your life back to him today. He'll give you exactly what you need to restore your relationship with him. Walking with Jesus will save you a lot of grief. That's good advice worth listening to.

LEAP

I know it sounds scary, but taking the time to talk to a friend headed for trouble is worth every bit of your time and effort. Before you do, I want you to be encouraged that you're doing the right thing. Here are some Bible verses that describe the qualities of a good friend and how to talk with someone struggling with sin. After you read each verse, write down how the verse applies to you and your friend. Before you meet with your friend, ask God for the wisdom to know what to say and the courage to communicate your unconditional love for your friend.

If one falls down, his friend can help him up. But pity the man who falls and has no one to help him up!

Ecclesiastes 4:10

So, if you think you are standing firm, be careful that you don't fall!

1 Corinthians 10:12

Brothers, if someone is caught in a sin, you who are spiritual should restore him gently. But watch yourself, or you also may be tempted.

Galatians 6:1

Dear friends, I urge you, as aliens and strangers in the world, to abstain from sinful desires, which war against your soul.

1 Peter 2:11

SENDING UP SOME AIR SUPPORT

LOOK

Let's face it: Some of your friends' problems are just too big, too complex, or too messy for you to be of very much help. As a youth minister, there have been times when I've felt completely inadequate or useless to help a student with those huge, life-changing problems that are out of my control. Break up with a girlfriend, I can handle that one. A fight with Mom or Dad, yep, got that one covered. But the biggies like death, divorce, or any other devastating tragedy I'm not as good at. For example, take my friend, P.J.

One Sunday morning, I walked up to P.J. and said in an enthusiastic, friendly voice, "Hey, P.J.! How's it going?"

Hanging his head low, P.J. mumbled, "Not so good."

"Yeah?" I continued. "What's wrong?"

P.J. looked up at me and said, "I just found out yesterday that my dad has terminal brain cancer."

Oh. Uh, wow. What was I supposed to say—"Gee, what a bummer"?

If you've ever been in one of those awkward situations where a friend of yours unloads a major problem bomb, you know how difficult it is to respond. What's the right thing to say? Should you even say anything at all? You sure don't want to say anything stupid. You don't want to make the problem worse or make your friend feel any more miserable.

You're not a psychiatrist or a professional counselor. Nor can you know the mind of God enough to give a perfect, spiritually correct response to explain why this sudden tragedy has happened. What are you supposed to do?

LISTEN

In the same way, the Spirit helps us in our weakness. We do not know what we ought to pray for, but the Spirit himself intercedes for us with groans that words cannot express.

Romans 8:26

If a friend of yours with one of those big problems confides in you, you don't have to feel inadequate, useless, or stupid in helping your friend. God's Spirit is going to help you help your friend. When you don't know what to say, the Spirit of God knows what to pray. You possess one of the most powerful, often overlooked, least understood gifts God has ever given to mankind. You have been given the gift of prayer. Even when you don't know what to say or even pray, God's Spirit will say it just right in a way that even words can't express.

Rather than looking for the right answer to give your friend, you can give him or her something they might not even ask for: prayer support. Call it prayer support, air support, it's the same thing. Just like Nike cushions their shoes with air-filled soles, you can help cushion the anguish your friend is experiencing by praying for that person. When you pray for your friends, you are sending them major spiritual air support.

As a fighter squadron provides vital bombing assistance to troops on the ground, your air support provides your friends with the protection and supportive shielding they need to make it through their battles. That's why the Bible tells you to pray continually. Prayer is one of the simplest, most practical, powerful ways to help your friends. You can't go wrong with prayer.

If a friend confides in you, don't look for the right answer. You may have it or you may not, but it's best not to gamble on your friend. He or she is looking for your friendship, your support, your encouragement. A right answer doesn't always provide the right kind of support, but prayer can stimulate your friend's faith to turn the situation over to God. Prayer doesn't provide you right answers; it provides you quick access to the God of all comfort. Just handing things over to God may be the comfort your friend needs most. That's something you can both do when you pray together. In prayer, you and your friend may not find answers, but you will find God. He's the answer to look for. He's the support your friend needs most.

LEAP

Do you have a friend who needs some air support? Do you know someone who's been going through a particularly hard time lately? While it doesn't seem like much, praying for your friends is one of the best things you can do for them. Sometimes, it's the only thing you can do. Take a few minutes today to pray for a friend. Ask God to be very real and present to your friend during this struggle. Ask God to give your friend his strength to trust in him. Pray for God to give him or her wisdom to make good decisions during this time of confusion. Pray for insight into how you can help your friend through his or her problem. Now, write a surprise note and let your friend know you're praying for him or her. It'll brighten your friend's day and remind him or her what a wonderful friend God has provided in you.

GETTING IN YOUR FRIEND'S FACE

"Kelly, the reason all of us are here today is because we love you and we really care about you. However, we refuse to allow you to destroy your life with some of the decisions you've been making lately."

This was not an easy meeting. Arms crossed, eyebrows slanted, and an intense frown on her face, Kelly sat back on the couch wondering what she was in for. Her body language screamed, "This is not very comfortable . . . why are all these people here?"

On the opposite blue couch, next to her parents, sat two of her closest friends, Mike and Jenny. Another friend, Steve, sat on a kitchen chair close by. Debbie, one of our girl staff leaders, sat with her legs crossed on the floor next to the couch. I sat directly across from Kelly.

"What we're going to do here, Kelly, is go around the room and let each person tell you how special you are to them." I paused. "Then, every person is going to explain in detail what they've seen going on in your life the past couple months. We all know you've been using drugs and alcohol, and that's why we're here. We don't want to see you destroy your life, your friendships, or your relationship with your parents. We're really concerned about you, and we're here to help you, but first you have to admit that you've got a problem."

For the next hour and a half of heart-to-heart truth telling, a lot of tears were shed; a couple of arguments ensued; some sensitive, brittle emotions surfaced; and a number of positive steps were taken to deal with Kelly's struggle with drugs and alcohol. Getting in her face wasn't very comfortable for her or for us.

LISTEN

Wounds from a friend can be trusted, but an enemy multiplies kisses.

Proverbs 27:6

How much do you love your friends? I mean, how much do you *really* love them? If you knew one of your friends was getting involved with drugs and alcohol, starting to hang out with the wrong crowd, stealing from stores and homes, thinking about joining a gang, suffering from depression, having premarital sex, thinking about committing suicide, going to run away, tagging (spray painting) freeways and businesses, struggling with an eating disorder, or bailing out on their relationship with Christ, you'd want to do something, right?

What would you do? Although it can be confrontational and intimidating, getting in your friend's face is one of the most solid ways you can show how much you love your friend. Loving a friend enough to tell them when they're blowing it or that they really need professional help is what real friendship is all about. Telling your friend the real truth about their life is radical friendship. The only problem is that a lot of times your friends think that they're invincible, indestructible, and immune to any sort of tragedy. *That'll never happen to me . . . I've got everything under control!*

Getting in your friend's face is clearly explaining to them that they're not in as much control as they think. It's one of the scariest and highest privileges you have as a friend. Jesus said that there's no greater love than a man who would lay down his life for a friend. Telling a friend what they *need* to hear, not what they *want* to hear, means laying down your life so your friend can experience real life. Confronting a friend means getting out of your comfort zone by yanking your friend out of his or her comfort zone.

Nobody likes to hear the truth when it hurts, but I'm afraid that too often we sacrifice the truth by wanting to be liked. When you tell a friend that their decisions stink, they get wounded and it stings. Especially when the truth is delivered by a close friend. But the Bible says that wounds from a friend are the types of wounds that can be trusted. Wounds from a friend are the wounds that God can heal. It's better to humbly, gently deliver a truth-filled wound than to suffer the loss of a close friend. And that's a radical risk worth taking!

LEAP

When we met with Kelly, we were very specific about what we hoped to accomplish. The following steps are for a serious intervention and they're not to be taken lightly. The most effective intervention meetings are led by someone who has proven experience leading them. Talk to a youth pastor, counselor, or older adult who can handle a crisis intervention in a professional and positive way.

1. Meet with the person's friends and family members.
2. Pray for wisdom and direction in leading the confrontation.

3. Clearly explain why you're meeting. You are here to deal with a serious problem.

4. Begin by having each person affirm your friend. Tell your friend why he or she is important to you and list the special qualities you see in him or her.

5. Then, have each person clearly explain the negative behavior patterns they've seen develop in your friend's life over the past few months or year. Focus on negative behaviors, attitudes, and actions; don't attack the person's character. Be clear and specific with times, dates, and situations.

6. Each person tells exactly how they feel about the friend's actions. (You hurt my feelings when you lied to me. I feel like I can't trust you anymore.)

7. Allow the person being confronted the chance to share their feelings.

8. Expect conflict and tears. This isn't an easy process. Stay levelheaded, stick to your game plan, and don't allow emotions to distract from the main issues.

9. Develop a game plan or action steps that your friend will agree to in order to change his or her behavior. This lets your friend know that he or she will have the support and encouragement from others to change.

10. Close your meeting with another round of affirmations. Have each person explain how he or she is willing to help your friend.

TOXIC WASTE FRIENDSHIPS

LOOK

Some friendships are a big waste of time, but that doesn't seem to bother some teenagers at all. Think about it for a second. A lot of things in this life get wasted that would drive any normal person crazy. What about when you waste seven bucks on a dumb movie you thought was supposed to be an action/adventure blockbuster hit? How about when you study a brain-warping chemistry chapter for two excruciating hours and later discover it was the wrong chapter? Or what about when you waste a month of your life being really psyched about the new girl you're dating, but out of nowhere, she dumps you? What a waste of time!

In high school, the type of waste I hated most was when I'd come home starving after practice, and the only thing in the whole house to eat was cereal, but there would be only an eeny, teeny, quarter inch of milk left in the bottom of the carton. I'd put the cereal in my bowl. I'd open the milk carton. I'd pour the milk and *whoosh!* Speeding out of the carton, the thin stream of white overshot the lip of the bowl, spilling all over the counter! Have you ever tried to eat cereal off a kitchen counter?

You can waste your hard-earned cash on a lame movie or waste your time chasing after girls who drop-kick you like half-eaten dogfood for other guys, but the most serious kind of waste in your life is hanging out with "friends" who are a waste of time. Friends who pull you down instead of up aren't real friends at all. They're toxic waste friends, and they have a half-life of 34,782 years.

I'm not talking about friends who occasionally mess up (because we all, at one time or another, mess up!), I'm talking about real losers . . . guys and girls who continually and incessantly tempt, challenge, and tease you to smoke, drink, cuss, tag, steal, cheat, or lie. If you're hanging out with friends like these, then you're either wasting your time or well on your way to a spiritual meltdown.

LISTEN

Greater love has no one than this, that he lay down his life for his friends.

John 15:13

Toxic waste friendships contaminate everyone in the surrounding impact zone. They stress out your parents, alienate you from your brothers and sisters, mess up your priorities, and can even dissolve your true friendships. Toxic friends would never even think to lay down their life for you.

Jesus said to be on the lookout for sneaky wolves in polyester lamb costumes. If you're careful to examine the attitude and lifestyle of a toxic friend, you'll find something doesn't look right. *I'm not sure what it was, but I think that guy had his mask on backward.* You can tell the difference between a real friend and a toxic friend. The person who's willing to lay down his or her life for you is the friend you want to find and follow. You need a friend to follow into battle, not someone who's setting land mines under your feet. Toxic waste friends spread their poison with how they live their life. When you smell something like rotten eggs, it's time to call the hazardous materials team.

Toxic waste usually ends up in one of two places: dumps and cemeteries. Toxic waste dumps are filled with leaking containers of acids, discarded nuclear chemicals, solvents, and old motor oil. Cemeteries hold many young people who, in some cases, wasted their lives hanging out with toxic friends. "That's a little harsh," you say. Oh yeah? How many teenagers' famous last words were, "It'll never happen to me." "I can handle what I drink." "Who needs a seat belt?" "I'm the only one who is a good influence on my friends . . . I can help them change." Do these lines sound a little too familiar? Who are you hanging out with? Are you wasting your time trying to impress a group of people who could not care less about you? Toxic friends will keep you inside your comfort zones and out of God's incredible plan for your life.

Leap

So how can you tell if you've got toxic friends or not? The Bible gives specific ways to identify the difference between real friends and toxic friends. How can you apply these qualities to your friendships?

"A friend loves at all times"(Prov. 17:17). We're not talking about a sappy, huggy-kissy type of love here, but the kind of love that's solid, strong, and committed to your best interests. This is God's vice-versa type of love for friends . . . it goes both ways. Toxic friendships are one-way friendships that go nowhere fast.

"Wounds from a friend can be trusted" (Prov. 27:6). A good friend will get in your face when you're blowing it. A good friend will bump you when you're outta line and do what it takes to keep you in line. A toxic friend would wound you for all the wrong reasons.

"If one falls down, his friend can help him up" (Eccles. 4:10). Friends pull each other up. Toxic friends knock you down. Toxic friends are often jealous, hyper-competitive, mean, and selfish. The type of friend you want will encourage you, strengthen you, support you, and help you to be the person God has designed you to be.

LONG-DISTANCE FRIENDSHIPS

Sage and Regan were the best of friends. An inseparable pair, they both loved singing, acting, and chasing guys. Regan's dad was a Christian record producer, and Sage's dad worked in radio production, so they often played characters in children's radio shows. They also recorded Christian music and went on cross-country ministry singing tours. Sage and Regan were filled with ideas, dreams, and plans for their budding singing and acting careers. Nothing was impossible for them. Together, they would conquer the world. Or at least conquer all the guys in the world.

One day Sage's dad came home with the awful, horrendous, terrible news every teenager dreads: "Pack your bags . . . we're moving." Sage's dad worked for a large Christian organization that was moving its headquarters to Colorado.

"Colorado!" Sage exploded. "What in the world are we going to do in Colorado? You guys go ahead without me because I'm staying right here!" Sage's sister, Erin, was even more livid. And diplomatic. Without her dad's knowledge, she wrote a letter to the president of the organization and asked him why he was trying to destroy her family and all her friendships.

Suddenly, all of Sage and Regan's bright dreams seemed to look dimmer. They had planned to attend the same high school, hang out with the same gang, and go on all sorts of youth ministry trips. But now, Sage and Regan weren't going anywhere together. Regan was staying put, and Sage was packing her bags.

LISTEN

Go in peace, for we have sworn friendship with each other in the name of the Lord.

1 Samuel 20:42

A fierce friendship can survive the toughest times, even a difficult move. But, if you've ever had to move away from close friends, you know things are never the same as they used to be. A friendship divided by a move can still stay strong, but by necessity, it has to change. In order for the friendship to survive, it has to be redefined. Sage just couldn't call Regan and say, "OK, I'll meet you halfway in Southern Utah. See you at the Dry Gulch 7–Eleven in ten hours."

An inexpensive local phone call becomes a monthly hundred-dollar long-distance phone bill. Creating memories with new friends tends to fade the old memories of your long-time friend. If a fierce friendship is going to stay vibrant and alive, both parties have to be committed to its survival.

Jonathan and David were two friends in the Bible who were split apart by a move. A sudden, desperate move. Jonathan's father, King Saul, hated David with an intense jealousy. He wanted to mow David down like an opossum in the road. Jonathan and David were best friends, but David had to flee for his life. Saul's anger became so intense that Jonathan had to dodge spears thrown at him by his own father.

Finally, Jonathan said, "Look David, my dad's crazy. You've got to leave town or he'll kill us both." Though Jonathan and David had spent years together, they weren't going to allow their friendship to be skewered by a spear. So what did they do? Filled with sadness and tears, these two guys who loved each other like brothers were really bummed. Slobbering and crying like babies, they got together and committed their friendship to the Lord before they said good-bye. That's not an easy thing to do.

In the New Testament, again and again Paul writes to his friends at all the different churches he's visited. He constantly tells them how much he misses them. He recalls how many times he's parted from them in tears. Paul reminds his friends how much he loves them and how he prays for them all the time. He's always praying for an opportunity to be reunited with them. Paul worked on maintaining his long-distance friendships. And he didn't have MCI, an Internet e-mail address, United Airlines, or the U.S. Postal Service to call, fly, or deliver next-day mail to his friends.

A friendship with God at the center is a friendship that is impossible to break up. Though things may be different, you can keep your friendship strong by committing it to the Lord and staying committed to keeping in contact. Letters, surprise phone calls, and visits during holidays and summer vacations can keep the fire of your friendship from burning out. Though it takes a lot more time and energy, a good friend is worth keeping. Even from a thousand miles away.

LEAP

If you've recently moved or had a close friend move away, how are you keeping your friendship alive? What can you do this week to show your friend you haven't forgotten him or her? What about someone in your youth group who has moved away? Get together with some friends and brainstorm ways to let the person who moved know he or she hasn't been forgotten. Create a video. Make a big banner and have everyone sign it. Call them up on a speakerphone and have everyone scream, "Surprise!" Take a collection and have everyone pitch in to buy them a plane ticket to come and visit. Plan a road trip to visit them. Don't forget to call ahead and let their folks know you're invading their house for the weekend!

FISH OR CUT
BAIT (SHARING
YOUR FAITH)

DROPPING EVERYTHING
TO FOLLOW JESUS

Look

As a freshmen boys cross-country coach for two years, my racing strategy was profoundly simple: R-U-N-F-A-S-T! Since only the top four or five guys on the team were the really strong runners, and the race results were based on their performance, my racing strategy changed for the ten or so slower runners on the team. My desire was just to see them finish the race to the best of their ability. If one of the slower guys broke his personal record by gutting out the three-mile race, it didn't matter if he was the first to cross the finish line or not. A new personal record was a new record. Victory was his!

My goal with my cross-country team wasn't so much to help teenagers win running races, but to win at life. And when playing to win at life, attitude makes all the difference in the world. So, at one of our first practices, I pulled out one of my favorite quotes and called everyone together.

"OK guys, listen up. Before we begin practice today, I've prepared some homework for you. Believe me, it'll make a big difference in all you do."

"Homework?" the guys asked, wondering what was going on. "What kind of homework could we possibly have for cross-country?"

"Public speaking," I replied. "Here is an 'attitude' quote that I want memorized by next week. Anyone who doesn't memorize it has extra miles to run. And, before you start your run today, I want you to stand on the bleachers and scream this quote out at the top of your lungs. I want everybody on the rest of this track to be able to hear you. I repeat, you cannot start your run until I and everyone else has heard you scream this quote."

In front of my team, the track field was swarming with other runners from the sophomore, junior, and senior teams. Including four teams of runners of the opposite sex! Here's their homework . . .

> I will never consider defeat and will remove from my vocabulary such words and phrases as quit, cannot, unable, impossible, out of the question, improbable, failure, unworkable, hopeless, and retreat; for they are the words of fools. I will avoid despair, but if this disease of the mind should infect me, then I will work on in despair. I will toil and I will endure. I will ignore the obstacles at my feet and keep my eyes on the goals above my head, for I know that where dry desert ends, green grass grows . . . I will forget the happenings of the day that is gone, whether they were good or bad, and greet the new sun with confidence that this will be the best day of my life.
>
> Og Mandino

Therefore, since we are surrounded by such a great cloud
of witnesses, let us throw off everything that hinders and
the sin that so easily entangles, and let us run with perseverance the race marked out for us. Let us fix our eyes on
Jesus, the author and perfecter of our faith, who for the joy
set before him endured the cross, scorning its shame, and
sat down at the right hand of the throne of God.

Hebrews 12:1–2

A few years after I left coaching cross-country, I bumped
into one of my former runners. Scott was now a senior, and
when he saw me, he immediately sounded off in a loud voice,
"I will never consider defeat and will remove from my vocabulary such words and . . ." Scott hadn't forgotten the
"homework" he had memorized three years earlier. He went
on to tell me how often the attitude quote inspired him to
never give up. My weird coaching tactics paid off well.

If you want to be an authentic, growing follower of
Christ, there are certain attitudes you must be willing to
drop and other attitudes you must be willing to develop in
order to walk with him. The first attitude you need to develop is to be willing to drop everything to follow Jesus.
Just like a cross-country runner wouldn't even think of
running with a backpack full of bricks, Christians need to
drop everything to run the race God has set before them.
Hebrews tells us to "throw off everything that hinders and
the sin that so easily entangles." What has hindered or en-
tangled your relationship with God lately? Throw it off.
Drop it now. Get rid of it.

Another important attitude that'll help you stay in spiritual shape is the attitude of refusing to give up on God.
Just like the quote says, remove from your vocabulary such
words as "quit, cannot, unable, impossible, out of the question, improbable, failure, unworkable, hopeless, and retreat; for they are the words of fools." No matter how tough
or confusing life gets, make up your mind today to never

run God out of your life. When some people get in trouble, instead of running to God, the source of all strength, they turn in the opposite direction and run away from him. If you're in trouble, run to God.

Still another attitude you want to work on is focusing your eyes on Jesus every day. Jesus is the author and finisher of your faith. He's the one who develops your faith and helps you to grow. Do you think Jesus is going to start his work in your life without intending to finish it? Fix your eyes on Jesus because he's cheering you on at the finish line waiting to catch you in his arms. He knows how hard it is to endure. He knows intimately what sweating and struggling are all about, but he never gave in to defeat. Because Jesus loved you so much, he refused to give up and quit. Even if things are really tough, when you drop everything to follow Jesus you can "greet every day with confidence that this will be the best day of your life!"

LEAP

What is keeping you from dropping everything to follow Jesus? What kinds of things have choked out your love for God? What occupies first place in your life instead of God? Confess your sins to God (1 John 1:9) and ask him to get rid of these anchors that are weighing you down. Fix your eyes on Jesus by studying Hebrews 12:1–14. Memorize the "attitude" quote and never give up!

BRINGING
YOUR FRIENDS ALONG

Rocky Brown (no relation to Charlie Brown or Rocky Balboa) is one of my high school heroes. A Christian high school student, Rocky is drenched with God's love, and he's not afraid to show it. He's convinced, sold out, committed, standing fast, and eager to let his friends learn how they can know his radical Lord. Rocky's not afraid to bring his friends along to meet the most important person in his life.

Rocky's a good football player, but he doesn't fit the typical football stereotype. He's not stupid. He doesn't have head cheese for brains. He's not so cool that he can't or won't talk to other students. Football isn't the only thing he thinks about. Though he loves the game, Rocky has other priorities too. Like letting his friends know what the first priority in his life really is: his relationship with God.

When Rocky was on the freshman football team, he wanted to score more than touchdowns for God. In fact, he was so fired up for God that he wanted to break all previous comfort-zone records. Praying for a way to reach his friends for Christ, Rocky talked with a local Student Venture youth worker to give a motivational talk to the football team. The end result:

Rocky and the youth worker began a Bible study for guys interested in learning about Jesus Christ. On the afternoon of the first Bible study, twenty-five football players packed Rocky's living room to hear about how to have a relationship with God. Rocky is the kind of high school student who knows that there's more to this life than just scoring touchdowns. He's a sincere, authentic Christian determined to help his friends find real victory in Christ.

LISTEN

Philip found Nathanael and told him, "We have found the one Moses wrote about in the Law, and about whom the prophets also wrote—Jesus of Nazareth, the son of Joseph." "Nazareth! Can anything good come from there?" Nathanael asked. "Come and see," said Philip.

John 1:45–46

High school students like Rocky inspire me to be a person eager to bring my friends along to meet Jesus Christ. You might be thinking, "Oh no! I'm not an evangelist. I don't know how to talk to people about God. I'm nothing like Rocky. I don't know what it is . . . I love God, but I'm afraid to talk to my friends about him."

If you feel intimidated about sharing your relationship with God with your friends, I've got a very simple answer for your faith-sharing heeby-jeebies: Just do what Philip did . . . bring your friends along.

When Philip met Jesus and Jesus asked Philip to come and follow him, Philip's first response was to go after his friend Nathanael.

"Hey, Nate, check this out! Guess who I met!"

Philip's natural enthusiasm for meeting Jesus spilled over into his friendship with Nathanael. Philip didn't start some big theological discussion. He didn't whip out any "turn or burn" pamphlets or hop on any soapboxes. He simply told Nathanael whom he had met and what he had experienced.

Nathanael jeered back at him with skepticism, "Yeah, right! Anyone from Nazareth is from redneck hickville. If you think the Messiah is coming from that dump of a city, you're crazy!"

Philip's response is something that will work for you today. All Philip had to say was, "Come and see. You check it out for yourself and decide." Philip knew that there was nothing he could do in his own power to convince Nathanael that Jesus really was the Messiah. That was Jesus' job, and the same is true today. As a Christian, you don't have to be the next Billy Graham to bring your friends to Christ. All you have to do is be willing to let them know *whom* you've experienced and bring them along in different sorts of ways so they can come and see who this Jesus really is. Yes, even bringing them along will get you out of your comfort zones, and your friends will be thanking you for eternity when you do.

LEAP

Bringing your friends along to meet Jesus can be done in lots of creative ways. The easiest way is to get them involved in your youth ministry by bringing them along on a trip or special event. Here are some great ideas that work to get your friends to come along to meet Christ. I've seen hundreds of students put these ideas in action, and you can make a difference in your friends' lives by doing the same!

Right where you are, you can be a youth ministry travel agent. Not only can you get your friends to go on great summer and winter camps, road trips, and mission trips, but you'll play a part in their eternal destination. Camps are fantastic opportunities for sharing your faith in Christ. The simplest way to bring your friend along is just to ask, "Do you want to ski insane moguls with two feet of untouched virgin powder? Do you want to help build a house for children? Learn to water-ski? Go on a ropes course? Meet a lot of girls?" All you have to do is get 'em to go on the trip. Let God's Spirit do the rest!

BECOMING GREAT
IN GOD'S EYES

Life presents too few opportunities to witness true acts of greatness. Fortunately for me, through a young man named Herb, I have witnessed tremendous acts of kindness and greatness in the eyes of God.

Let me explain: Herb was not the type of guy on campus known for being a witty comedian or an outstanding athlete. He wasn't very popular or handsome according to what some teenagers consider popular and handsome. Herb, in strictly high school terms, was none of those things. By most high school standards, he was an outcast. Herb was confined to a motorized wheelchair by cerebral palsy. Hunched over from more than fourteen back operations, Herb operated his wheelchair with twisted, tightly clenched fingers. His speech was barely intelligible, making conversation extremely difficult. Drool spilled out of his mouth when he flashed his great, friendly smile. Though Herb had friends in his special education class, he had few friends elsewhere. He wasn't the type of socially acceptable friend you or I would go looking for.

I saw student after student, though, make Herb feel welcomed and accepted at our Wednesday night outreach ministry, Student Body. Student Body was a place for students to bring their friends to hear the gospel. Student Body had wild games, burger bashes, pizza nights after football games, snow skiing, waterskiing, and rock-climbing trips in order for our staff and students to develop new relationships with other teenagers. Herb had come to Student Body because someone handed him a flyer at school and told him it was a good place to meet new friends. Instead of getting shunned like he often did at school, Herb became a Student Body regular. How often do teenagers with cerebral palsy experience acts of greatness like these:

- Five guys carried Herb and his two-hundred-pound wheelchair up a steep, tight staircase to get him to Student Body. (Don't tell his mom!)
- Students befriended and stayed with Herb when they probably would have rather sat with their other friends.
- During our burger bashes, students patiently sat with Herb and fed him his hamburger and drink.
- On car rallies, teenagers would hop into Herb's specially equipped van instead of taking off in their friends' cars.

LISTEN

Not so with you. Instead, whoever wants to become great among you must be your servant, and whoever wants to be first must be your slave—just as the Son of Man did not come to be served, but to serve, and to give his life as a ransom for many.

Matthew 20:26–28

In the life of a wonderful, smiling young man with cerebral palsy, I witnessed teenager after teenager serve Jesus in disguise. Every time I saw a young person go out of his or her way to grab Herb a drink or a hamburger or serve whatever need he had, I witnessed the heart of Jesus in action. These students served Herb before themselves. They didn't worry about what their friends thought. They were more concerned with what both God and Herb thought.

James and John were two of Jesus' disciples with "me first" attitudes. Total mama's boys. Their mom, who probably still dressed them, came to Jesus with a Godzilla-size request. Wanting her precious babies to sit at Jesus' left and right in heaven, she got the other disciples riled up about who would sit where in heaven.

"Guys! Guys! Guys! Settle down, settle down," Jesus cried out. Then he set them straight: If you want to be great, become a servant.

Becoming a servant for Jesus is not something you'll hear about on *Entertainment Tonight*. You probably won't make the six o'clock news or win the Nobel Peace Prize. But, if you get out of your comfort zones and serve others, you'll be great in God's eyes. By serving others, people will see your faith in action and wonder what makes you tick. That's when you'll be able to tell them it's not a "what" that moves you to action but a "who." That "who" is Jesus Christ. There are lots of ways to serve other people. You don't have to know someone with cerebral palsy to begin. But if you do know a student with special needs at your school, that's a great place to start. An incredible way to crunch your comfort zones is to give your life away to others.

LEAP

Jesus came to serve and give his life as a ransom for many. Who are the people on your campus who need a friend? What about a loner in your youth ministry? Serving others is a practical way to demonstrate your faith. Remember: People may not remember your words, but they will remember your life. Become great in God's eyes by serving others. People like Herb will thank God for eternity for people like you.

FISHING FOR YOUR FRIENDS

LOOK

When I was a little kid, one of the highlights of my life was the YMCA Indian Guide program. My dad was "Big Lightning," and I was "Little Lightning." On one of our Indian Guide pow-wow excursions, our tribe headed to a muddy beach ranch somewhere along the coast of Baja California. I don't remember much about the weekend except that it was raining, we couldn't ride the horses, the food stunk, and it wasn't exactly one of those John Wayne adventures I loved on television. However, there's one thing I'll never forget.

My dad loved to surf fish, and on this rainy Saturday, I tagged along with him down to the beach, wearing my little leather Indian vest. Some of the other kids were playing on the shore, but I wanted to watch my dad fish. He got his pole all ready, baited the hook, and began walking into the cold water to cast his line. As I goofed around on the shore, I didn't see him bring the pole over his shoulder, ready to launch the line into the water.

All of a sudden, a burning, piercing, stinging sensation seized my right thumb like someone had just lit it on fire. I quickly looked at my thumb. Stuck right in the middle of it was a bloody fish hook. In a split second, my tearing eyes followed the path of the hook, which was tied to the fishing line, which was attached to the fishing pole, which was held by my dad's hands, which were ready to cast my thumb out to sea.

With all the fear and terror I could muster in that miserable millisecond, I took a deep breath and screamed, "AAAAHHHHH!!!"

My dad had just caught the biggest tuna of his life. He looked over his shoulder and saw his hook stuck in my thumb. He also discovered that this little Indian wasn't too excited about his fish hook initiation rites.

LISTEN

As Jesus was walking beside the Sea of Galilee, he saw two brothers, Simon called Peter and his brother Andrew. They were casting a net into the lake, for they were fishermen. "Come, follow me," Jesus said, "and I will make you fishers of men." At once they left their nets and followed him.

Matthew 4:18–20

One of the most powerful examples of a true disciple of Jesus Christ is a young person who is willing to leave everything behind to follow Jesus in order to become a "fisher of men." As a Christian, your life is bait, fresh bait, for the kingdom of God. Jesus wants your life to attract people to himself, and as his disciple, fishing for your friends is one of the most important ways to help them discover who God is. Fishing for your friends can be done in all sorts of creative ways. Here's what two high school guys have done to help bring their friends to Christ:

Jake's an extreme type of guy. The kind who does insane, crazy sports and likes to live out his faith in the same way. Jake and a friend started "Rock-N-Ride," an outreach ministry to share their faith by taking friends rock climbing and mountain biking. Wouldn't *you* pray to Jesus if you were hanging off an eighty-foot cliff by a skinny rope?

Jaime is an actor and dancer who recently went on a tour with a group called the Young Continentals. Part of the tour swung through his town, so Jaime invited his friends to see the performance. Hot music, good singing, cool dancing, and funny skits shared God's message in a creative, fun way. When it comes to his friends and God, Jaime ain't acting.

When you go fishing for Christ, Jesus promises to lead you in everything you say and do. You are the bait, and his love is the hook. The great thing about God's love is that there is no sting.

LEAP

All it takes to influence a friend for Christ is asking a few simple questions. Yes, it's risky, kinda scary, definitely out-of-the-comfort-zone business. It's not exactly like talking about the Bulls or Blue Jays, but asking a good question in an open, nonjudgmental way can help your friend consider meeting their most important friend: Jesus. Here are some creative questions to help you and your friend talk about heavenly, spiritual matters in a down-to-earth kind of way.

1. What's the most important thing in your life? Why?
2. Who do you admire the most? How come?
3. Can I tell you about the person whom I admire the most and why?
4. If you were going to die, would you rather freeze or burn to death?
5. What bugs you the most about death?

6. Do you think there's life after death?
7. Who is the closest person to you that's died? Where do you think they are now?
8. Do you believe in heaven and hell?
9. What would you do if everything you own was stolen or destroyed?
10. If you were to die, how many people would come to your funeral?
11. What do you think it means to be a Christian?
12. What would you want written on your tombstone?
13. What do you think God's favorite basketball team is?
14. Have you ever been to church? What was it like?
15. Who do you think Jesus is?
16. Do you ever pray? What do you pray about?
17. Have you ever had any prayers answered? In what way?
18. If you were God, what would you do to fix the world?
19. If you wanted to get to heaven, what do you think you'd do?
20. What's the meanest, worst thing you've ever done?
21. Why do you and I do rotten things?
22. Are people basically good or evil?
23. How do you think bad people get to heaven?
24. Why do so many people wear crosses? What does the cross mean to you?
25. Do you believe Jesus died on a cross? Do you think he rose from the dead?

SHARING WHO YOU KNOW

LOOK

Sharing your faith in Jesus Christ just may be the most difficult comfort zone you ever break. Someone asks you about God, and you freeze. You don't know what to say. Cold sweat drips down the back of your shirt. Your mouth gets pasty and dry. Your pulse hits warp speed. Your face turns pale and your head begins to feel a little light. How do I know? You're not alone . . . there are thousands of teenagers who've experienced this same terrifying out-of-body experience.

For the past ten years, I've conversed with countless teenagers who've put an enormous amount of pressure and guilt on themselves when it comes to telling their friends and family about Jesus. Sharing their faith in Christ is just about the scariest thing they can think of. If that's you, then you've probably struggled with these kinds of guilty thoughts:

I should be more bold in my faith. If I really love God, I shouldn't be afraid to talk to my friends about God. I should be more like Mike . . . he talks to everyone about the Lord. I should have said something about God to Susie when I had the chance.

Instead of enjoying God's presence and having their faith be a natural expression of what God is doing in their lives, too many students paralyze themselves with guilty minds filled with "should've's, would've's, and could've's." If sharing your faith scares the stomach bile out of you, it could come down to some very real fears: (1) Fear of rejection: Maybe my family will think I'm really weird. Will my friends like me if I tell them that I love God? (2) Fear of not saying the "right" thing: What if I get confused and my friend totally rejects God because I say something wrong? I have doubts all the time about my faith, so how can I possibly convince others? (3) Fear of not knowing enough: What if someone asks me, "Do dinosaurs go to heaven?" What if I'm asked to prove the existence of God? What will I say? (4) Fear of looking really stupid (now you're talking!): What if someone compares me to a Hairy Kristian or some other weird cult? What if the subject of Christianity comes up in class and I sit next to a really cute girl?

I don't want to minimize the importance of being able to tell others about Jesus Christ, but at the same time, I don't think God wants you to be consumed with guilt and confusion about sharing who you know. Read on!

LISTEN

Then the righteous will answer him, "Lord, when did we see you hungry and feed you, or thirsty and give you something to drink? When did we see you a stranger and invite you in, or needing clothes and clothe you? When did we see you sick or in prison and go to visit you?" The King will reply, "I tell you the truth, whatever you did for one of the least of these brothers of mine, you did for me."

Matthew 25:37–40

Sharing your faith in Christ is important, but words are only one way to communicate the gospel. People will understand who Jesus Christ is when they see the character of God lived out in your attitudes and actions. In the story of the sheep and the goats, Jesus makes it very clear that it is our actions that count most: feeding the hungry; giving a cup of cold water in the name of the Lord; taking in strangers; clothing the naked; visiting the sick and the prisoners. People will remember you most for your actions, not your words. Nowhere does the Bible make a big deal about how eloquent or smart you have to be to communicate your faith. Look at some of the heroes of the faith: Moses had a stuttering problem. Peter had terrible timing and his mouth always got him in trouble. Jeremiah said, "I'm too young . . . what am I supposed to say?" Paul said his preaching did not come from "wise and persuasive words" (1 Cor. 2:4). What separates the sheep from the goats is the demonstration of God at work in our lives through our actions and not necessarily our words.

What you lack in clever arguments, insightful thoughts, or clear gospel presentation skills, the one area no one can challenge or dispute you in is a transformed life. If God has truly gotten hold of your life, then sharing who you know begins through your actions. You see, sometimes I think we make Christianity out to be like a crazy circus filled with poodles jumping through flaming hoops. We feel as if we need to perform for God. We should know more, say more, do more. God already loves you for who you are, and Jesus has already told us the things you need to do to share who he is to others. Remember: Christianity is all about a *who* and not a *what*. Sharing who you know begins with a transformed life. You may not know the answer to every question that's thrown your way, but who knows? Maybe we will see dinosaurs in heaven.

LEAP

Instead of placing a lot of "shoulds" on yourself, how about focusing on areas in your walk with God that you really want to grow in . . . areas where you *choose* to grow. Instead of saying, "I should talk to Bob about God," try saying, "I'm going to ask him if he wants to come to youth group with me." Trade a lot of your negative thinking about things you think you *should* do with practical, simple ways to live out your faith . . . things you *can* do. Is there someone in your neighborhood who could use your help this week? Are there any elderly people whose lives you can cheer up with a simple visit? What about helping out at a soup kitchen or ministry for the poor? Trade in negative thinking for positive, faith-filled action. Sharing your love for God can be done in simple, practical ways that'll lead people to ask you who inspired you to do such things in the first place.

SHAKING,
BAKING, AND
BREAKING THOSE
COMFORT
ZONES

LAYING DOWN YOUR LIFE
FOR A FRIEND

LOOK

"Come on . . . get in the car . . . we're not gonna wait here forever so you can figure out if this is a good moral choice or not. It's only a small party . . . you can call from Kim's bedroom when we get there . . . it's no big deal," your best friend pleads as three other guys squished in the back-seat stare at you as if you were wearing a pink ballerina tutu. A small party. You've heard that one before.

This is the third time in a month that the plans have "suddenly changed." Your best friend's canned lines are becoming vaguely familiar:

"If I would have known earlier, I would've told you so."

"Going to the drag race wasn't my idea . . . it was Pete's!"

"How was I supposed to know there was going to be booze at the party?"

"Listen . . . nobody forced you to come with us . . . you could have said 'No.'"

Your friend's life is going down the drain. Down the toilet. Right into a stinking sewer. You smell it. You feel it. You see it. You know it. It doesn't take a rocket scientist to figure out what a stupid decision looks like, but what do you do when your friend's initial one or two stupid decisions have now developed into a negative lifestyle?

What are you supposed to do when the buddy you've hung out with for the past few years doesn't like hanging out with you anymore? OK, maybe he won't admit it, but you can tell he's real careful about what he says around you now. When you ask him what he's doing this weekend, he: (A) avoids the subject; (B) says he hasn't decided yet [which means: (1) He's lying, (2) He's keeping his options open, (3) He's blowing you off, or (4) He's embarrassed to say he has to go to his grandma's]; or (C) tells you he's already made plans with Scott, which automatically XXX's you out of the picture, since your friend knows that you won't hang out with Scott, because you know what Scott's all about. How can you help your friend see that he's blowing it? What can you do to win him back from his new "friends," who don't give a rip about him?

LISTEN

This is how we know what love is: Jesus Christ laid down his life for us. And we ought to lay down our lives for our brothers.

1 John 3:16

Jesus was betrayed with a kiss from someone who was supposed to be his friend. There are a lot of Judases today, and chances are you'll find one or two in your friendships during junior high and high school. Your friends may not be collecting thirty pieces of silver, but stuff like drugs, al-

cohol, sex, drag racing, gossip, adult movie channels, stealing, tagging, cheating, and lying to parents are all like
subtle, seductive, warm, tempting kisses. First your friend
wants one . . . then another . . . then another. Before your
friend knows it, you're both a long way from Kansas, and
Toto's nowhere in sight. Are you a true friend or a Judas?
Are you going to lay your life down for your friend or roll
over and play dead?

The night Jesus was betrayed by Judas and deserted by
his closest friends, he told them something I'm sure they
never forgot: "Greater love has no one than this, that he
lay down his life for his friends" (John 15:13). Even
though Jesus' friends abandoned him, Jesus still laid
down his life for them. That's radical! When you put
what you think and feel about talking to your friends
aside and actually go and talk with them, that's laying
down your life for your friends. When you value your
friends more than your awkwardness or feeling stupid,
you are living out the sacrificial love of Jesus. That's laying down your life with love. That's breaking your comfort zones for God. That's nothing to feel embarrassed
about . . . just ask Jesus.

LEAP

Ten Tips for Tackling
Tough Talks with Friends

I believe your friendships can make or break your relationship with God. They will help make or break your comfort zones. I've seen too many young people abandon their
friendship with God for friends who later abandoned them.
Friends like that ain't worth it. Don't trade God for your
friendships. Don't trade Jesus for the world. Instead, as an
ambassador for Jesus Christ, lay down your life for your
friends. Here are some simple ideas that *can* work, *might*
work, and I pray *will* work for you.

1. Don't preach . . . your friend needs a real friend, not a parent or a pastor.

2. Make it clear that you're not condemning; just concerned enough to bring up a subject your friend probably would rather not talk about.

3. Be specific. Don't refer to vague situations. Present clear facts that are based in truth, not rumor or exaggerations.

4. Avoid words like *always, never, every,* and so on. They sound too extreme and can make it seem as if you're talking down to your friend.

5. Find a good place to meet that will be free of distractions.

6. Be willing to own up to situations/conflicts/inconsistencies about your own life that your friend may bring up. Honesty is a good bridge builder.

7. Focus on your feelings rather than your friend's failures. He's already going to feel awkward enough without someone beating it into him.

8. Brainstorm ideas on things to do instead of partying and getting into trouble. Help your friend create some fun alternatives.

9. Be ready to go the distance with your friend. Everything probably won't change in one meeting. Be willing to meet again and again.

10. Pray for your friend and ask God to give you the strength to put your friendship in his hands!

CUTTING OUT
CONFORMITY

Do you remember playing with Play-Doh as a kid? Packed in a bright, rectangular yellow box with five round cans of white, yellow, green, red, and blue hunks of squeezable soft dough, Play-Doh was the favorite creative goo for child-size imaginations. You could squeeze, punch, pound, flatten, and mash the doughy stuff into all sorts of colorful creations. Roll it into snakes. Make little people and animals. Taste it. Chew it. Throw it. As a master Play-Doh creator, you could manipulate and conform the dough into any shape you liked. If you bought the Play-Doh Factory, you got to use it like Mom's pasta maker, squeezing the dough into stars, circles, triangles, and all sorts of other shapes and sizes.

As a teenager, you and Play-Doh have a lot in common. First, you both have a high salt content and neither of you tastes very good. Second, there are all sorts of forces trying to squeeze, mold, and conform you into a shape different than God's original design. You are bombarded with pictures about the perfect body shape. Your mind is pressed

to believe lies instead of truth. Your friends can squeeze you out of their circle if you don't dress and act like they do. You can be made to feel like a square for taking a stand for God. The distinction between right and wrong is squished by the belief that everything is relative . . . that there really are no rights or wrongs. And like the Play-Doh Factory, the world wants to squeeze you out and cut you into little pieces with a plastic knife, so you conform to the same size and shape as everyone else.

LISTEN

Therefore, I urge you, brothers, in view of God's mercy, to offer your bodies as living sacrifices, holy and pleasing to God—this is your spiritual act of worship. Do not conform any longer to the pattern of this world, but be transformed by the renewing of your mind. Then you will be able to test and approve what God's will is—his good, pleasing and perfect will.

Romans 12:1–2

It's easy to feel like an insignificant chunk of Play-Doh while trying to be a Christian in this world. You constantly get the snot squeezed out of you. If you don't conform to whatever's in at the moment, you're made to feel like something's wrong with you. "Oh, you're still a virgin?" "You make it sound like everyone who drinks gets killed in a car accident!" "If cheating helps me get into a better college, what's wrong with that?"

Breaking your comfort zones for God's kingdom means breaking the mold this world wants to set you in. God has a better way for you to live your life, and Romans 12:1–2 shows you how: (1) As an act of pure worship to God, offer your body to God as a living sacrifice. No, you're not going to spill your guts on some eerie, blood-drenched altar. Your heart, mind, and soul are yielded to God's standards and purposes for your life. (2) You refuse to go through the Play-Doh Factory. You don't follow the pattern of this world. You choose to be a unique individual designed by the Master Creator. You don't conform like dough in a cookie cutter to what everyone else is doing. (3) You allow God's Spirit to transform you by renewing your mind. Instead of mindlessly following others, you think about and test things and try to figure out God's will for your life. In that process, you discover the importance of reading and knowing about God's expressed will found in his Word. You think new thoughts about God and others. Your outlook on life is fresh and original. Your ideas on how to live for God stimulate new spiritual growth in your life.

The amazing result is discovering how satisfying it is to live according to God's will. His divinely designed will for you is good, pleasing, and perfect. As a unique, treasured member of God's family, his gentle hands want to shape and design your life into a priceless masterpiece.

LEAP

Be a kid again, go out and buy some Play-Doh. If this seems too silly to do on your own, tell your youth pastor to buy some. Use it in a youth group meeting to talk about Romans 12:1–2. Make your own creations illustrating how the world wants to shape you in its image. Contrast that with creating something God wants to shape in your life. Use the Play-Doh as a fun teaching tool to discover how Jesus Christ wants to transform your thoughts and actions. Play with some with your friends. Ask God to help you live by his standards and not the world's.

GETTING RID
OF *STINKING* THINKING

A playground is no place for arguing and fighting. Playgrounds are supposed to be places for having fun. My favorite playground is Joshua Tree National Monument, and it's the place where I love to go to climb rocks and enjoy God's incredible creation. Unfortunately, on one of our high school rock-climbing adventures to Joshua Tree, I found myself in a heated confrontation with an obnoxious attitude lodged in the brain of a high school freshman named Jake.

After a blistering-hot day of belaying students up and down gargantuan rock boulders the size of six-story buildings, a couple of volunteer leaders and I headed back to camp to make some lemonade. As Michelle and I were mixing the cold water and throat-choking lemonade powder, Jake walked up and barked, "Hey, when's that stuff gonna be finished?"

"In a few minutes. Pull up a rock and relax," we replied.

A couple of minutes later, Jake snapped again, "Aren't you finished yet? I'm thirsty!"

Jake was now pressing my You-Are-Annoying-Me button. I was tired, sunburnt, and having him spew his unappreciative attitude all over the place wasn't exactly the type of soothing relief I was looking for.

"Chill out, Jake! It'll be done in a minute," I responded with my You-Are-Annoying-Me tone of voice. A couple of other people also told Jake to give it a rest, but Jake was restless. He was not picking up our hints of social displeasure. Minutes later, Jake returned to sample our unfinished, watered-down lemonade.

"This stuff is weak! Don't you guys know how to make lemonade? Whatsa matter, Joey? Can't you read directions?"

That's it. Enough. Code Red. DEFCOM 5. Missile Alert.

"Jake, your attitude stinks. Leave. All you're doing is complaining, and I'm sick of it. I want you outta here right now!"

Jake stood his ground, saying defensively, "Can't you guys take a joke?"

I shot back, "Not with an attitude like yours. Now leave. I'm serious."

LISTEN

Finally, brothers, whatever is true, whatever is noble, whatever is right, whatever is pure, whatever is lovely, whatever is admirable—if anything is excellent or praiseworthy—think about such things. Whatever you have learned or received or heard from me, or seen in me—put it into practice. And the God of peace will be with you.

Philippians 4:8–9

Jake didn't handle his attitude too well in that situation. Neither did I. He could have chosen to politely ask for

lemonade, like he learned back in kindergarten, but he
didn't. He chose an attitude that was negative and selfish.
I could have chosen to be patient, like I learned back in
kindergarten, but I didn't. I chose an impatient, trigger-
happy, missile-launching reaction to his volley of rude re-
quests. Both of us were uncomfortable, tired, and thirsty.
We both thought: *He's the one being a jerk.* Neither of us
wanted to budge an inch outside of our comfort zones.

To break out of your comfort zones, you need an attitude that can survive the pressures of living outside your
comfort zones. Just as a diver has to decompress after experiencing the crushing atmospheric pressure of deep-sea
diving, a good attitude helps you to decompress after the
challenging pressure of breaking your comfort zones. When
you're outside your comfort zones, you face tremendous
gravitational forces that want to pull you back inside before God has finished his work in you.

A negative attitude is stinking thinking that will keep
you from being all that God has designed you to be. You
can only become what God wants you to be when you
allow his Spirit to help you break your comfort zones.
Stinking thinking will keep you inside that warm, womb-
like comfort zone of self-absorption. That's why Paul offers such a wonderful suggestion for thinking the types of
thoughts that can give you a new view of God, others, and
yourself. What does Paul say? He tells us to think about
things that are true, noble, right, pure, lovely, admirable,
excellent, and praiseworthy. Then, while you're thinking
about these things, put them into practice!

Instead of criticizing the lemonade, think about thanking those who made it. Instead of reacting to someone's
bad attitude, look beyond their words and find something
admirable in that person. When your attitude is in the right
place, your actions will follow. What does Paul say the
benefit of trading in stinking thinking for a Christ-like at-

titude is? "And the God of peace will be with you." That's exactly what Jake and I needed most!

LEAP

In my office, where I sit and write all these crazy stories, there's a quote by Chuck Swindoll above my desk that constantly challenges me in my thinking about God, others, and myself. I hope it helps you as much as it does me.

> The longer I live, the more I realize the impact of ATTITUDE on life. ATTITUDE, to me is more important than facts. It is more important than the past, than education, than money, than circumstances, than failures, than success, than what other people think or say or do. It is more important than appearance, giftedness or skill. It will make or break a company . . . a church . . . a home. The remarkable thing is you have a choice every day regarding the ATTITUDE you will embrace for that day. We cannot change our past . . . we cannot change the fact that people will act a certain way. We cannot change the inevitable . . . The only thing we can do is play on the one string we have, and that is our ATTITUDE. I am convinced that life is 10 percent what happens to me and 90 percent how I react to it. And so it is with you . . . You are in charge of your ATTITUDES.

What kind of stinking thinking do you struggle with? How can you put Paul's words into practice in your life today? What does this quote tell you about how to handle your attitudes?

GETTING NAILED

If Tiffany Daniels only knew. All semester long you've stared at her pretty brown eyes, long golden hair, shimmering white teeth, and heart-stopping smile, but you've been too chicken to ask her out. *She'd never go out with me*, you mourn to yourself. You know you lack the needed charm, studly body, clever wit, and all the other required credentials, including money, to get her to go out with you. You have nothing to offer her. *Except* . . . you have something Tiffany needs: your brains.

You spent all last night studying for your history test. Shunning your favorite TV program, you meticulously memorized every significant event, important name, and bloody battle of the Revolutionary War. Confidence overflows in every step you take as you march into third period, goose-stepping toward your seat. Your brain is loaded, armed, and ready to fire away at every multiple-choice, fill-in-the-blank, matching column, vocabulary definition, and essay your teacher launches at you. You are ready for war.

Sitting down, you glance over at Tiffany and say, "Hi! Ready for the test?"

Pouty and teary-eyed, Tiffany slowly turns toward you and says softly, "No, I'm probably going to fail. I studied for so many hours, but all these people and dates and battles just confuse me. If I don't pass this test, I'll have to go to summer school. I don't know what I'm going to do." She folds her arms on her desk and buries her head in frustration. *Aha! . . . Time to make my move! Time to earn some major extra credit from her!*

LISTEN

If we confess our sins, he is faithful and just and will forgive us our sins and purify us from all unrighteousness.

1 John 1:9

You thought your teacher was out of sight. You thought you'd never get caught! Wrong! You failed to realize that teachers have a highly sensitive sixth sense for smelling conspicuous conspiracies like cheating. You forgot that the classroom door has a little rectangular window used for looking out and looking in. You weren't looking out. Your teacher was looking in. You didn't hear the classroom door open. You felt a sudden lurking, sinister presence behind you. It was chilling. Eerie. Suspicious. Only after the vise-like squeezing sensation of your teacher's hand crushing your shoulder; the crackling, sheering sound of your test being shredded into papier-mâché; and the sharp, stern clip of your teacher's voice saying, "Mr. Snodgrass, I'd like to speak with you and Miss Daniels immediately after class," did you realize that you were truly, unsuspectingly nailed.

Instead of copping a bunch of lame excuses that make no sense to anyone but you, the first, best, and hardest thing to do is admit that you've been nailed. In other words, plead guilty. That way you can head right to the trial and sentencing. Attempting to blame others, avoiding responsibility, or adjusting the story to make you or the incident not look so bad only drags the problem out. And that's a bummer for your mom, teacher, friend, or coach, the very people you don't want to upset any more than they are. Admitting you're wrong is the first step to resolving the chaos you just created.

The next step you want to take is accepting the consequences for your actions. You see, you may be willing to admit you've been nailed, but accepting the consequences for what you've done is a much bigger step than a lot of guys are willing to take. Consequences are a part of the real world and accepting consequences means paying for what you've broken, apologizing for what you've said or done, and accepting any punishment for your crimes against humanity. OK, maybe just crimes against your sister.

Lawyers, parole officers, and bail bondsmen can give you all sorts of legal counsel on getting nailed, but the best advice for when you get nailed comes from 1 John 1:9. Why is confessing your sins and receiving forgiveness from Jesus Christ the best advice? After accepting the consequence of being sentenced to your room until next winter, there still may be the possibility that you've got unfinished business with God. That's where confession comes in. Confession isn't just admitting, and it's not just accepting. It's agreeing with God that you're wrong. You can admit and not agree . . . and you can accept responsibility and still not agree. Confessing means a wholehearted, 100 percent, unconditional agreement that God is right and you are wrong. Confession is admitting, accepting, and agreeing. The whole enchilada.

Though he was innocent, Jesus admitted, accepted, and agreed with God that something had to be done for all the stinking sin in this world. Jesus Christ, the son of the living

God, was beat up, bruised, and bloodied for your sins and mine. His crucifixion cost him his life and you nothing. No matter what you've done, you can freely confess your sins to him. He is faithful and just and will forgive you. He didn't get nailed for nothing. Jesus got nailed for you.

LEAP

Confessing your sins and mistakes to God restores your relationship with him. Confession breaks your comfort zones and strengthens your relationship with Jesus. Before you do anything today, take some time to confess your sins to God. Don't allow anything to block your relationship with him. Receive the forgiveness and freedom that are freely given in Christ by admitting, accepting, and agreeing with God about your sins. Don't let sin gouge a hole in your heart. Getting nailed gives you the chance to get right with God.

BREAKING YOUR
COMFORT ZONES

We had just waded through a wide, knee-deep river and hiked a short hill to arrive at the South American jungle prison. We were led by two missionary friends to *la granja* (workfarm), a Bolivian prison that held sixty inmates ranging from petty thieves to drug dealers to murderers. What surprised me most was that some of the prisoners were almost half my age. Ranging from ages thirteen to fifty, the workfarm prisoners suffered unsanitary living conditions, malnourishment, and torturous beatings. Walking into the dark, putrid, filthy living quarters, my eyes snapped a desperate mental picture of human suffering at its very worst.

Crowded on steel-frame beds with no mattresses, the prisoners stared at us with bruised, gaunt faces. Infected, seeping, open wounds from fights or beatings from the prison guards covered their bruised bodies. One prisoner lay on his bed moaning in agony from broken ribs suffered during a fall from the cable carriage that crossed the river. Covered with a white coat of plaster-type material, the scabbed legs of three prisoners were punctured with hundreds of insect bites. Long, ugly scars. Short, scissor-chopped haircuts to prevent lice from nesting. Wheezing and coughing from infected-lung colds. Dark, empty eyes. The reeking smell of body odor and human feces overwhelmed our sanitized American senses. If this wasn't a living hell, then what on earth could it be?

Banished from their families, cut off from the rest of society by dense, remote jungle, what hope could prisoners living in such pathetic conditions ever have? Who or what could ever ease their misery and pain, their desperation?

LISTEN

Then they cried to the LORD in their trouble, and he saved them from their distress. He brought them out of darkness and the deepest gloom and broke away their chains. Let them give thanks to the LORD for his unfailing love and his wonderful deeds for men.

Psalm 107:13–15

As he did on every weekly visit, my missionary friend, Phil, began to share the good news of the gospel. Preaching in the darkness of the cold, ugly prison walls, Phil told the story of Jesus hanging on a cross with two criminals. He told the prisoners how God loves criminals, people who have abandoned not only the laws of God, but the laws of society as well. Phil explained how Jesus came to set all people free from the heavy chains of their sins that separated them from God. Sitting on the steel-frame bunk beds bunched in groups of four and five, the prisoners listened intently. No one but Phil ever regularly visited the workfarm prison. Like Jesus Christ, Phil was one of the few people who really loved these men. He was the only one who offered them the forgiveness of sins, a restored relationship with God, and eternal hope through Jesus Christ. God was using Phil to break the chains of sin and death.

Visiting the prison workfarm shattered my comfort zones of sleeping in a soft bed, eating good food, and living in a safe place free of torture, disease, and abuse. Experiencing the visible, horrible living conditions of the prisoners gave me a picture of what separation from God really looks like. The prisoners' physical condition gave me a vivid picture of what my spiritual life without God really is: Gloomy. Desperate. Dark. Painful. Hopeless. Hell.

Because of Jesus Christ, I've discovered countless reasons to thank God for his unfailing love. More than anyone I know, God has proven his wonderful deeds and faithfulness to me over and over again. How about you? Have you experienced the tremendous, wonderful freedom found in God's unfailing love for you? Have the chains of sin and death been broken in your life? Have you discovered friendship with God through Jesus Christ? Are you willing to have your comfort zones broken so you can enjoy God's presence in your life every day? If so, then you're well on your way to being God's person.

Breaking your comfort zones is a daily choice, a firm resolve, and a determined stance to be God's person wherever you are. It's choosing God's way over your way or the world's way. Breaking your comfort zones is an intentional step to walk with Jesus every day of your life. It's a lifelong process of following him wherever he leads you.

LEAP

Jesus broke the power of sin and death over our lives through his life, death, and resurrection from the dead. On the cross, he broke his comfort zones so you could experience a restored relationship with his Father. If you haven't given your life to Jesus Christ, there's no time like right now to let him begin his work in your life. All you have to do is pray, "Father, forgive me for my sins that have separated me from you. I confess my need for you, and I ask that you give me new life through your son Jesus Christ. Holy Spirit, come into my life and make me the person you want me to be. Give me your strength to be ready and willing to break any comfort zone that would keep me from you and your love. In Jesus' name, amen." If you've prayed that simple prayer, welcome to God's family. You are a new creation in Christ, and God promises to help you grow in your new relationship with him.

If you've already made a commitment to Christ, why not take some time to read over Psalm 107. Take a pen and write down all the wonderful things God has done for you. Write down everything you are thankful for in Christ. Keeping a thankful attitude, even during times of hardship and discouragement, will definitely keep you out of your comfort zones. Being thankful will keep you focused on Jesus, who was bruised and broken because of his great love for you.